COPING WITH

A BIGOTED

PARENT

Maryann Miller

THE ROSEN PUBLISHING GROUP, INC./NEW YORK

Published in 1992 by The Rosen Publishing Group, Inc.
29 East 21st Street, New York, NY 10010

First Edition

Library of Congress Cataloging-in-Publication Data
Miller, Maryann, 1943–
    Coping with a bigoted parent / Maryann Miller.—1st ed.
      p.   cm.
    Includes bibliographical references (p.   ) and index.
    Summary: Examines bigotry, the problem of living with a bigoted parent, and ways to adjust to such a situation.
    ISBN 0-8239-1345-7
    1. Children—United States—Attitudes—Juvenile literature.
2. Toleration—Juvenile literature. 3. Discrimination—United States—Juvenile literature. 4. Prejudices—United States—Juvenile literature. [1. Prejudices. 2. Discrimination.
3. Parent and child.] I. Title.
HQ772.5.M55 1991
303.3'85—dc20
                                 91-32739
                                     CIP
                                     AC

Manufactured in the United States of America

ABOUT THE AUTHOR ◇

I n over ten years as a journalist, Maryann Miller has amassed credits in a number of national and regional publications, including *Lady's Circle, Byline, Sunday Woman, Marriage and Family Living,* and *Plano Magazine.* At *Plano Magazine* she also served as editor from 1983 through 1986. She has also been published in major Dallas newspapers as a columnist, reviewer, and feature writer. Currently, she is a Public Relations Consultant for The Catholic Foundation, which is the largest Catholic endowment institution in Texas.

Her educational background is in sociology and psychology, and she continued that interest by volunteering in social programs through her church. Many of those programs involved teenagers, whom she admits she enjoys almost as much as a good pizza.

Married for over twenty-five years, Ms. Miller is the mother of five children, ages sixteen through twenty-four.

Acknowledgments

Although my name is on the cover of this book, the credit belongs in a real sense to all the people who provided me with assistance. My special thanks to my good friend Jimmy Hudson, who so willingly shared his experiences with me and allowed his story to be so much a part of this book.

Also deeply appreciated are all the young people who trusted me with their own stories. Not only was it extremely helpful, it was a most enjoyable experience to spend time with you trading ideas and opinons.

Others who assisted with factual information include members of the Anti-Defamation League, "A World of Difference," and the wonderful resource librarians at the Plano libraries.

And finally, thanks to my family. Once more you came through with the kind of support I needed to complete this book. What would I do without you?

Contents

Introduction

If civilization is to survive, we must cultivate the science of human relationships—the ability of all peoples, of all kinds, to live together in the same world at peace.
—Franklin D. Roosevelt

For some people, Roosevelt's sentiments may seem an impossible ideal to achieve. As a society, we have spent decades excluding certain groups because of racial, religious, or ethnic background, and too many people still consider it right and justifiable.

But now more than ever, as we move further and further into an era of "global dimensions" when our neighborhood is no longer limited to the people who live on our block or in our community, we have to break down the barriers that separate us.

The hope for the future shines on you who have already been growing up with an enlightened vision. Your attitudes may have been fostered by your parents so that you have never really struggled with a conflict of opinion about bigotry. If so, you are very lucky.

Or perhaps you count yourself among the many whose views differ from those of their parents. Maybe you have grown up in a household led by bigoted attitudes and have struggled to overcome them in efforts to treat all people with dignity and equality.

Maybe you are still struggling. It is not necessarily a war that is won with a single battle. It may last your entire lifetime, depending on how strong your parents' bigoted attitudes are. But you are not alone, as you will discover in reading this book. Young people all over the country are responding to the awareness that a world without bigotry is a better place to live. And the effort will make a difference.

Martin Luther King, Jr., the great civil rights leader of the 1950s and '60s, believed that justice and equality would come when people were no longer separated by fear and uncertainty. It would come when the white community no longer saw the black man as a threat, but was able to see him as a person. Then the oppression would stop.

That was the beginning of my own awareness as I confronted the prejudicial attitudes I had accepted without question from my parents. I became uncomfortable with my feelings toward others based on unsubstantiated stereotypes: Blacks are to be feared because they are mean and aggressive; Jews are not to be trusted because they will take advantage of you.

What I came to realize was that some people are mean and aggressive, and some people will take advantage of you, but they do not have to be black or Jewish to be that way. People are people, and we owe each individual the opportunity to be seen for who he is, not for what group he belongs to.

The following was written by Martha H. Reed to the Letters to the Editor column of the Dallas *Morning News*, and it sums it all up neatly: "Americans are not a race—they are a people. We are all races, all cultures and all bloods. This philosophy must be faced once again in all its beauty if we wish to unite and overcome this revulsion of feelings [racism] which is now devastating us."

CHAPTER ◇ 1

You Are Not Alone

When Jimmy Hudson was only five years old he was aware that racism was not right. He did not know specifically what racism meant, of course. He was much too young to grasp that kind of concept. But some inner prodding told him that the ugly, hateful remarks he often heard from other family members were wrong.

Bigotry was strong in Jimmy's family, but strongest in his maternal grandmother, who considered herself an aristocrat. Because of her position in the upper class, she simply believed she was better than most people, especially blacks and Hispanics. She ran a household with a number of servants and never hesitated to voice her bigotry in front of them. Jimmy can recall her making remarks at the table while the maid was serving dinner.

Although his grandfather occasionally spoke up in defense of the people Grandmother attacked, most of the family accepted it. But it always made Jimmy uncomfortable.

One day when his other grandmother said something racist about blacks, it bothered Jimmy enough that he told his father later, "Colored people are as good as I am."

Jimmy's father thought it was funny, and later at a large gathering he told the rest of the family. One uncle laughed and said, "Well, you may think they're as good as you are, but Maumi certainly knows they're not as good as she is."

The remark was soon to become a family joke, constantly repeated, and being the object of that kind of joke created problems for Jimmy. He was very hurt and embarrassed every time they laughed at him, and he is sure that the embarrassment affected him for a long time. "Many times later in life, I refused to stand up against racial remarks," he says, "and it was because of that personal embarrassment."

When the incident happened, Jimmy had no idea how he understood what he was saying or where it came from. "It came strictly out of the blue," he explains. "The only remarks about race or religion I had ever heard in my life were negative. I had never heard anything sympathetic. So I feel like I created that myself somewhere."

From that first moment of awakening, Jimmy continued to develop beliefs that were contrary to those of his family. "They were contrary to the community I lived in, too," Jimmy points out. "This was a well-established upper-class neighborhood. Racial and religious bigotry were widely accepted."

Jimmy recalls an incident when he was playing football with some other guys from school. He was about fourteen at the time. "We were scrimmaging, I think," Jimmy says, "and one of the guys muffed a play. One of the other guys yelled at him, 'You stupid Kike!' Then he turned to another guy who was Jewish and said, 'I didn't mean you. Just him.'

"I'm not sure why he said that to the other guy," Jimmy

continues. "But I can remember feeling deeply hurt by what he had called my Jewish friend."

It was the ugliness of the remark that bothered Jimmy. He explains that every time he heard a racist remark he felt the same way, hurt and embarrassed. "Certain kinds of comments can be just as much of an evil gesture as an act of aggression."

Often, as Jimmy grew older, he wondered how most of the family could continue to believe the things his grandmother said. She continued to promote negative stereotypes even though it was clear to him that her reasoning was all wrong. Why couldn't the rest of them see the flaws in her thinking?

One obvious flaw became apparent when Jimmy's grandmother's maid died. She had worked for his grandmother for forty years and had not saved money for her funeral, so his grandfather had to pay. His grandmother was quick to point that out as a example of how irresponsible blacks are: She couldn't even take care of her own funeral. "But what Grandmother failed to point out," Jimmy says, "was that they only paid her fifteen dollars a week. How could she have been expected to save any of that?"

His grandmother was not only unjust in what she said about her servants, she was also totally oblivious to any sense of inequality in life-style. After the maid's death Jimmy went with his grandfather to the servants' quarters behind the house. It was the first time he had ever been inside, and he was horrified at the room the maid had lived in. "It was so tiny," he says. "Small does not describe it. It was incredibly tiny compared to this great big house my grandmother lived in.

"But those things were simply ignored," he continues.

"There was no thought of injustice. It was simply the way things were."

By the time Jimmy was in high school, he had developed his own racial values that were contrary to most of the rest of his family. His mother had inherited her mother's tendency to make ugly remarks, and seldom did anyone try to correct her, not even Jimmy.

Part of the reason he didn't speak out was that when he did he was usually ignored. He was considered too liberal in his thinking on most issues anyway, so no one took him seriously.

The other part of the reason is something that Jimmy is not particularly proud of. "I simply didn't have the courage to say anything," Jimmy says. "I'll never forget how embarrassed I was that first time, and I didn't want to be embarrassed again.

"You also have to understand that this was not an everyday issue. I continued to be hurt and confused every time something negative was said, but we never had confrontations over it. When I started to speak out more, it became a situation where they knew that when something was said that I objected to, I was going to reply. And they were going to reply, ignoring whatever I said. Then we would just get on with life."

Throughout his college years, Jimmy came to realize that he couldn't change his parents or grandparents. Sometimes, because of their bigoted attitudes, he felt an inner conflict over love and loyalty and all the things that make up family relationships. He had lost respect for their thinking and had to find some balance to keep the relationship intact.

Perhaps it is a testament to the strength of the family bond that they could "agree to disagree." Although Jimmy never accepted the values he considered wrong, he learned to separate them from other family issues. The family, likewise, never accepted Jimmy's liberal views, but they tolerated them.

"There were too many other good things about our family life that overshadowed that one negative thing," Jimmy explains. "And there were lots of things I could respect about my family. This one issue didn't have to alienate us."

The closest they came to alienation was when Jimmy married a Jewish woman.

After graduating from college, Jimmy had gone overseas to take care of family business, and it was there he met Claudie. It didn't matter to the family that she was French, but it did matter that she was Jewish. "I had not realized until then how strongly anti-Semitic they were," Jimmy says. "No one in the family came over for the wedding."

For the first few years Jimmy and Claudie lived overseas, so the problem could simply be ignored. But when they came back to the States it was awkward.

Jimmy's sister and brother accepted Claudie readily, but there was a lot of reserve among others in the family. "They weren't hostile about it," Jimmy explains. "But I do remember Dad's being terribly disappointed that my wife and kids were Jewish. I knew it wouldn't change anything if I said, 'What difference does that make?' but that's what I wanted to say. That's what I believed."

Now, many years later, things are a little better. Most of the older folks who openly promoted bigotry are gone, and there is more family unity. Sometimes it bothers Jimmy just a little that his family never fully accepted his having different attitudes. It also bothers him that he was unable to effect a change in them, but he's enough of a realist to know that you cannot change another person.

One thing that pleases Jimmy considerably is that his

father has mellowed in his attitudes over the years. It did not have much to do with Jimmy's influence, however. It was because his father's life experience changed. In time, Jimmy's father came to see Claudie the person separate from her religion, and his perspective changed. "I wish I could take credit for it," Jimmy says. "But he changed only because he was able to find out for himself all the qualities that make Claudie a good person."

Jimmy's lifetime experiences with bigotry have given him an acute awareness of injustice and all its evils, and he is a firm believer in equality. The little boy who said, "Colored people are as good as I am," still dictates much of Jimmy's attitudes and actions toward people of other ethnic groups.

The advice he would like to give to you who may be having similar experiences is to have the courage of your convictions. Stand by your principles and speak out against racism of all kinds. It is the only way these issues will be resolved.

Jimmy knows it isn't easy. He still recalls painfully the many times he lacked the courage to challenge a racist remark. "There were too many times I didn't speak out," he says. "To my parents. To other kids when I was young. To businessmen when I was older. And I really regret that.

"But I can't dwell on past mistakes. I have to try to do the right thing today. Right now. And even though it sometimes still scares me, I always feel better when I do."

CHAPTER ◇ 2

Who's a Redneck?

Prejudice takes many forms, and the degrees of prejudice vary.

James, a twenty-year-old college student from Houston, says he was in the sixth grade when he first realized that his father was bigoted. "It started with jokes," he says. "Then he would make ugly comments. He never told me I couldn't bring my black friends home, but he sure made it clear he didn't approve."

When James got a little older he tried to suggest to his father that maybe it wasn't right to joke around the way he did, but it made no difference. "Most of the time he just ignored me. It was as if he just didn't get the point."

Now James finds that he has less in common with his father than he did when he was younger. Mostly it is because of the differences in their attitudes, and James wishes it did not have to be that way. But he knows that wishing won't change anything, so he just keeps on working to improve his own attitudes.

James admits that he had some prejudicial attitudes. "I think everyone does to a certain degree," he says. "But when you realize you have them, you have to do something about it."

One of the things James is doing is trying to be really open to the wide range of ethnic groups on his campus. "I used to be more reserved with other groups," he says. "Now I've been trying to get to know some of the Hispanic and Asian students. It's really made a difference."

Kelly*, a twenty-one-year-old college student in Missouri, has had a similar, yet stronger experience with family bigotry. Her father is extremely prejudiced. She says that even though she understands how he came to think that way, it doesn't make it any easier to live with the problem.

"His attitudes were formed by his childhood in the South," she explains. "There, blacks were okay as long as they stayed in their place. Anyone who didn't was seen as a troublemaker. My father grew up during the volatile days of early civil rights activities, and he was influenced by all of that. Then the years he spent as a street cop in California only reinforced it.

"I would try to tell him it wasn't fair to think that all black guys were like the ones he was busting," Kelly continues. "But he just couldn't see it."

Kelly remembers that even when she was very young she would get angry when her father made ugly remarks about blacks. Maybe they were watching TV and he would make fun of a black performer. She would try to tell him to stop and they usually ended up yelling at each other. Finally she would just leave the room when he started, but it still made her angry. As she grew older, she found she was terribly disappointed in her father. It was as if he had somehow let her down because he refused to consider that he might be wrong.

Kelly is not sure how or why she has different attitudes

* Name has been changed.

than her father. In fact, most of her family are prejudiced, so it is a mystery why their influence didn't make her prejudiced as well.

Some of the how and why has to do with personality types. Studies have shown that distinct characteristics set prejudiced personalities apart from tolerant personalities.

RECOGNIZING BIGOTS

Extreme bigotry is easy to spot. It is usually very open and without question as to purpose or intent. Members of white supremacy groups such as the Racist Skinheads or the Ku Klux Klan are very vocal about their beliefs. Because of that openness, it has been easy to study the personality types most likely to hold extreme bigoted attitudes. Less is known about the people who have what some consider "acceptable" forms of prejudice.

Many people see no harm in telling a few jokes, or standing up for your rights against people exerting their rights. They justify their position by saying, "Hey, it's not like we're hurting anyone. We haven't taken up arms or kept someone from getting a job. We're just getting a few laughs."

Yet those same people are often outraged at violent expressions of racial prejudice. They voice their disapproval loudly, sometimes even using it to justify themselves further. "You want to talk about prejudice, that's *prejudice*. We haven't bombed any churches lately."

These people fail to see any connection between their attitudes and those of the extreme bigots, and they might be surprised if you were to suggest that they were prejudiced.

Clint, a nineteen-year-old college student in Texas, thinks that may be true of his parents. "They just have some old-fashioned attitudes," he says. "Sort of condescending . . . if you're not white, you won't make it."

Clint says that for a while he pretty much went along with his parents. He had no reason to question what they said. Then at some point his attitude started to change. He is not sure when, but he is sure it was the result of his physical challenge. He was born with spina bifida and is paralyzed from the waist down. "I know it broadened my perspective," he says. "I don't like to see anyone put down or made to look inferior because of factors they can't control."

People who are strongly prejudiced have certain personality characteristics in common. Many of them are rigid and inflexible. They look for status and power in relationships with other people, and they have low self-esteem.

Some sociologists have identified this kind of people as "authoritarian personalities." They often come from families characterized by harsh and threatening parental discipline. As children, they tend to be very insecure and feel unconscious hostility to their parents. Without help in coping with their feelings, they usually grow up to be angry adults.

A 1948 study of prejudiced children found that most of them held the following beliefs:

- There is only one right way to do anything (rigid and unyielding).
- If a person doesn't watch out, somebody will make a sucker out of him (insecure, unreasonable in fears).
- It would be better if teachers were more strict (shifting responsibility).
- Only people like themselves have a right to be happy.

• There will always be war; it's part of human nature.

The same study applied to adults produced similar results. The conclusion was that a prejudiced person often acts from an underlying insecurity. The person cannot face the world without fear, and he has to rationalize and justify that fear.

Even though the study was done so long ago, it still defines some of the major characteristics of prejudiced personalities. It seems that not much has changed in human nature through the years. Perhaps you can even recognize a few people who fit those characteristics:

Johnny, who has been in school with you since second grade and always argues about everything. Sometimes you swear he would argue that the sky is green and the grass is blue if someone tried to tell him otherwise. He seems to need always to be right, even when he's wrong.

Sarah, who always complains that she can't get her work done because the rest of the class is making noise. If only the teachers could keep things under control, she would be able to get better grades. Somehow she manages to ignore the fact that she doesn't always do her homework, which has more to do with her poor grades than the noisy class. But she doesn't want to accept responsibility for herself. It is easier to make it someone else's fault.

Bob, the new guy who wonders why you're being nice to him. You must want something. Nobody is nice just to be nice. He figures you are just setting him up for something, a joke maybe. People do that all the time.

To gain even more insight into the prejudiced personality, let's look at the other side.

TOLERANT PERSONALITIES

Like prejudice, tolerance is seldom the result of a single cause. It is the result of several forces that influence people throughout their lives. If the forces all support the same values, they reinforce each other.

What shapes us during childhood is a combination of temperament, family atmosphere, specific parental teaching, and school and community influences. All those factors affect us as we grow up and determine what kind of adults we become.

Tolerant people usually come from homes with a nurturing atmosphere. As children, they feel welcome, accepted, and loved no matter what they do. In their homes there is a sense of certainty about action and reaction. The child need not be on guard all the time. There is a security of knowing where he stands even when he makes a mistake. Love and affection are not used as bargaining chips.

That security is a key element in a tolerant personality, according to Gordon Allport, author of *The Nature of Prejudice*. It is the opposite of "threat orientation," which is often found in the background of prejudiced people.

Without that sense of threat, tolerant people are less rigid and more understanding of the "human condition." They do not get so upset about other people's mistakes, nor do they usually go crazy about their own mistakes. They have a good sense of themselves as worthwhile individuals and often handle responsibility better than intolerant people.

Allport lists other characteristics of a tolerant personality:

1. Good companionship and fun are regarded as more important than good manners and "proper" behavior.

That does not mean that manners are thrown out the window and we do whatever we want, which is more indicative of a self-serving personality. But a person with a tolerant personality is more concerned about guests having a good time at a party than about how the house looks. That indicates an ability to be aware of other people's needs over your own. As mentioned before, prejudiced people are very self-centered.

2. Rejection of a two-value logic.

Prejudiced people often see things in terms of either/or. For them, issues are seldom seen in shades of gray. Tolerant people tend not to be so limited. To them, there is a vast array of considerations between black and white. They do not believe that "There's only one right way to do anything," and they seldom put people in categories.

3. High frustration tolerance.

Tolerant people are often categorized as easygoing. They don't get upset over delays or misunderstandings. When things go wrong, they don't find it necessary to blame others.

Such people can make you feel good just to be around them. They seem so calm, so centered, and usually so optimistic. They are the kind of people you would like to seek out when you have a problem; just their attitude helps put things in perspective.

4. Positive respect for individuals.

Some people have a true spirit of goodwill toward others. They see strangers as potential friends rather than a threat, and they are often interested in cultural differences. They have a strong sense of justice and seek fair treatment and equality for all people. They feel comfortable in groups different from what they are used to.

At a party with a new group, they don't hang back waiting for someone else to make the first move; they are open and friendly with everyone.

5. Liberal political views.

Liberals tend to favor nonrevolutionary progress and reform. They also tend to take an optimistic view that human nature can be changed for the better. Sometimes they are labeled naive and unrealistic, sort of like Don Quixote who tilted with windmills. But without such people it would be a world full of cynics. We could give up trying to make things better.

6. Empathy.

Tolerant people seem to have a greater ability to see people for what they really are. They are often more accurate in their judgments of personality than are intolerant people. The ability to see people realistically allows the tolerant person to avoid friction in relationships. He can trust his own instincts and does not feel apprehensive or insecure about others.

7. Self-insight.

People who know themselves well and are comfortable with that knowledge, good and bad, are less apt to blame others for what is their own responsibility. They admit it when they are wrong and accept the consequences. Likewise, they recognize their talents and gain great confidence from using those talents to achieve a goal. They do not get sidetracked with irrelevant fears or concerns.

It might be interesting now to go back to Jimmy Hudson and see how these characteristics fit.

At first glance you might think he gets a zero on the nurturing family bit. After all, his family were very prejudiced and did not respect his opinions. But because personal security is such an important element in the ability to form different views, it is clear that Jimmy had to be very secure about himself. Even though his family never *accepted* his opinions, they *respected* him. They never told him that he was less of a person because of his opinions, and they never told him he couldn't have them. They just chose to ignore them.

In the areas of empathy and respect for individuals, without doubt Jimmy has those qualities. The fact that he cared so deeply about incidents and insults that were not even directed at him surely proves that. Even his managing to find a balance between rejecting his family's prejudice and still accepting them shows the degree of his respect for people.

Jimmy is also a man of great self-insight. When he admitted his faults and shortcomings, he offered no excuses nor did he try to diminish them in any way.

Likewise, when he spoke of his good qualities he did so without bravado. Everything was simply stated as fact without an overwhelming sense of pride. That is simply the way he is, and he is very comfortable with all aspects of his character.

Throughout his narrative it was also clear that he is a person who sees all sorts of gray areas in life. He is definitely not rigid or limited in his thinking.

Does that mean that Jimmy has reached some superhuman level of tolerance? Not really. He certainly is further along than some people, but he is nowhere near perfection. To him, the highest level of tolerance would be having no ethnic attitudes at all. "People would have no interest in group distinctions. A person is just a person. No color, religious, or cultural designations to set us apart."

That is a sentiment expressed by many people, and I think we can all recognize it as the ideal. It is a goal we can set for ourselves with the understanding, and acceptance, that we all will fall somewhere short of the ideal.

No matter how enlightened we think we are, we all have a little prejudice. It does not matter what race or ethnic group we belong to, we have a tiny instinctive response to some situations that overrides our intellectual response.

On the surface we recognize what is unjust or unfair because of what we know, but our reactions can be influenced by so much more.

To illustrate that, let's do a little self-assessing.

Imagine this: A black teenager is driving through a white neighborhood and a cop pulls him over. The cop says the guy was speeding, but he denies it. Then the cop makes the guy get out of the car, frisks him, and makes him wait in the squad car while he checks him for priors. It turns out the young man has a clean record, so the cop releases him after issuing a ticket.

In court the young man files a complaint that the cop treated him unfairly. He says he was only going a few miles over the limit, which he thinks was not enough for the cop to stop him. He also thinks the cop should not have frisked him or made him sit in the squad car.

The cop defends himself by saying that the fact the young man was in an all-white neighborhood was suspicious enough to justify stopping him. He says that his other actions were based on sound principles resulting from experience. If the young man had been up to no good, leaving him in his car would have allowed him to escape.

Think about that scene, and ask yourself the following questions:

- Do you think the cop was justified in stopping the young man?

- Was the cop's suspicion based on racism, or a judgment based on experience?
- Given the same circumstances, do you think the cop would have pulled the guy over if he had been white?

A similar scene was used for a program on "A World of Difference" that aired on WFAA-TV in Dallas in 1990, and audience response to the questions was varied. The audience was a balance of ethnic groups, and not all groups responded as expected.

Some whites agreed with blacks that the cop was racist, but not all blacks thought he was. A small percentage of people in all the groups thought there was some justification for the cop's suspicions. Another small percentage thought the cop would have stopped a white teenager if something dictated by experience gave him sufficient reason.

In an analysis of the test and its results, it was suggested that in a world totally free of prejudice maybe there wouldn't have been any questions to ask. Maybe the whole incident would have been accepted as simply the cop's doing his job. Nothing else would have been read into it.

Looking at it from another angle, maybe the cop would not have stopped the young man because there would have been nothing suspicious about a black man's being in a white neighborhood.

No matter how you answered the questions or what you think of some of the other opinions, you can see that no one is totally one-sided on such issues. You can also see how easy it is to be prejudiced for or against certain things. It is part of human nature.

We are never going to change human nature, but we can

change what we think and how we act. We can question our responses to situations and make sure they are valid, not knee-jerk responses. We can also try harder not to read more into a situation than is really there.

If we all do that—not just a few, but all of us—we can go a long way toward achieving racial harmony.

CHAPTER 3

Why Stay a Redneck?

With most people, prejudicial attitudes remain in the background most of their lives. The attitudes exist but are not a major factor in day-to-day activities. Nor do they usually act on them openly. James's father never goes beyond the jokes, and Kelly's father seldom does more than make ugly comments.

But given the right circumstances, these same people can become as vocal and active as the most fanatical bigot. Why? Because they feel threatened.

The most obvious threat is *violence*. During the race riots of the 1960s people on both sides of the issue did things they probably would not have done under other circumstances. A white man in Detroit kept vigil with a shotgun. Although he had never before thought of using it against another person, he was ready to do so to defend his family.

A young black man who lived in a mixed neighborhood went back to his parents' home until the rioting was over. He was afraid of reactions from whites in the new area, even though they had all been getting along fine until then.

A high level of emotionalism swept over the whole city of Detroit during the rioting and turned people inside out. Many of the people responsible for the looting and burning were just ordinary folks. They were not hardened criminals or even past troublemakers. They were just people reacting to a threat.

Another threat is *economic*. When facing high unemployment or a financial recession, people tend to become very self-protective. As long as there are jobs to go around, it's fine to have a few black guys on the job. But the minorities become the enemy when the unemployment lines are long.

One factor that certainly influenced your parents' generation was *affirmative action*. It was an effort to hire and promote minority workers with an eventual goal of reaching an equitable balance between white and minority workers.

Idealistically it was a good program, with sound reasoning to sustain it. Unfortunately, the implementation of affirmative action often fell short of the ideal. The only equality achieved was the equality of blame for its ineffectiveness.

Many whites who were extremely bigoted fought the concept at every turn, sometimes resorting to open hostility and harassment. That reaction only proved to the minorities that they were right, "They still think they're better than we are. They'll never accept us."

On the flip side of the responsibility coin, some black workers took advantage of affirmative action. One white man in Michigan remembers an incident from the early '60s. He was nineteen at the time and had just gone to Detroit to work as a carpenter's apprentice.

"We only had a few black folks in our little town, and I don't suppose we ever really had an attitude about them. I don't remember Dad or Mom ever saying anything against them.

"Personally, I thought they were okay. They were good people, hard-working. And I guess I just never thought much about the difference of color.

"So it was no problem for me when the foreman told me one day that he couldn't hire my nephew as he had said he would. He explained about this new 'quota' thing, that he had to hire a black guy instead.

"So, okay. I wasn't thrilled. My nephew needed the job, but it would have been the same had the foreman hired another white guy. At least that's what I thought at first.

"Then after a week or so I noticed that this black guy wasn't pulling his fair share. All the apprentices had to do the drudge work—haul the lumber and tools for the rest of the crew. But that black guy wasn't doing it. Every time I turned around he was taking a break.

"Well, I figured once the foreman caught on, that guy would be gone. No work, no pay, was sort of the way we looked at things then.

"After a while, when it seemed as if the foreman wasn't noticing, some of us went to talk to him. He told us he couldn't fire the guy. It didn't matter that he wasn't doing his work and was fouling things up for the rest of us. He had job security, and there was nothing the foreman could do about it.

"Yeah, I can tell you about affirmative action, but it's not fit to print in your book."

What happened to that man was not the way it worked everywhere. Plenty of black workers *didn't* abuse the system. But because some did, it created an attitude and a widespread generalization: "Those blacks are simply taking advantage of us. They don't really want a good job. They just want to be paid for nothing."

Frustration is another thing that keeps prejudice alive. Frustration is a widely recognized motivator of unreasonable thoughts and actions. We often direct our frustration at whatever is convenient instead of the true cause of the emotion. It happens in all kinds of situations, even at home.

You come in from school one day and Mom climbs all over you because your room is a mess. It has been a mess all week, but she didn't say a word until today. Why did she wait so long to get mad at you?

What you have no way of knowing is that she is mad at the repairman who never showed up after she had waited all day. She is frustrated and angry. Unfortunately, you were the first one to cross her path and give her an outlet for her feelings.

People do that to each other on large and small scales every day, and prejudice feeds on it.

Studies have shown that the tolerance level of frustration among prejudiced people is lower than among the nonprejudiced. Most of us learn to control our reactions to frustration. We seldom resort to venting our anger through physical violence. Occasionally we give in to an impulse to yell or scream or throw something. That's natural. But as we mature, we curb our impulse to have temper tantrums. We learn to vent our anger appropriately.

Part of the reason highly prejudiced people don't reach that balance has to do with personality type. Because of their insecurity and tendency to be inflexible in their thinking, their actions are often somewhat immature.

Our normal responses to frustration also vary. The most common reaction is an attempt to overcome the cause of frustration. We are having trouble finding the sources we need for our research paper. Even though we may feel a bit panicked, we are still determined to find them and get the paper done. Our frustration may even increase our energy level, making us work harder to track down the books we need.

If second and third efforts still leave us without what we need, we may resort to other responses. Sometimes we blame others: "That stupid library never has what I need."

Sometimes we get angry, wad up our paper, and throw it across the room. "I quit! I don't care any more. I'll just get a zero."

In a natural progression though these stages of frustration, we often end up back at the beginning. After ranting and raving for a while, getting it out of our system, we settle down to look for another way to overcome the obstacle.

Another factor that certainly influenced your parents' generation was the television show "All in the Family." Archie Bunker became *the* stereotype of a redneck, and because the comedy was so good, it somehow made him more acceptable.

Although the show did make some valid points about the prejudiced personality, it also perpetuated some myths. Because Archie never changed, no matter how many new ideas and experiences he was introduced to, it gave the impression that bigots never change.

That is not true. Bigots change all the time. Not because *we* change them, but because something in their life influences them to change. It does not happen quickly, as Jimmy's story points out. It took years for his father to come to some realizations for himself. But it did happen, and it can happen again.

The other myth promoted by "All in the Family" was the belief that all bigots are stupid. Many of them are uneducated, but they are not stupid.

Archie Bunker's stereotype was not the result of lack of

intelligence as indicated in many episodes of the show. It was a composite of all those factors that influence our development that we looked at in Chapter 2.

Using those factors, let's give Archie Bunker a little more reality:

Temperament

Archie was rigid and limited in his thinking. He was also very self-centered and self-absorbed. Seldom did he relate to other people with empathy or understanding.

He was also judgmental and negative in his attitudes toward others, yet he seldom looked at himself with a critical eye. Everything bad that happened was always someone else's fault; he was always right and everyone else was wrong.

Family Atmosphere

Because his family was portrayed as lower middle class, they were probably hard-working, believing that everyone can get ahead if they work hard enough. They were also probably not very well educated. There would not have been many opportunities for Archie to be exposed to new ideas. Family conversations revolved around matters of survival as opposed to world or social affairs.

Specific Family Teaching

Because of limited experience with the reality of the problems faced by minorities in our society, Archie's family fell back on the attitude that somehow it was the fault of the minority. When and if they felt threatened by a minority, they accepted the widespread attitude that they were the enemy.

Archie certainly could have been influenced by the common generalizations of the time. "What do they have to cry about. They're free, aren't they?" "They're just trying to take advantage of us."

School and Community Influences

At that time the schools taught little or nothing about black history. Blacks were mentioned in American history as part of the period surrounding the Civil War, but even that was a narrow view. There was seldom any mention of blacks outside of slavery issues, which severely limited white students' awareness of blacks.

The community influence was just as limiting. As was common in neighborhoods of that time, people clustered together and supported common values. The men who sat on the front stoop after dinner talked about the problems they had with minorities at work. The kids playing stickball in the street accepted what the older men said as gospel. That is how it worked then, especially in areas where there was little formal education. Nobody questioned anything.

With that in mind, if you were to watch some reruns of "All in the Family" perhaps you could look beyond the laughs and see that Archie Bunker is a bigot. Perhaps you could also gain some insight into other bigoted personalities.

A factor that contributes to prejudice in a more subtle way is the pattern of striving for success that characterizes American middle-class life. From the time many of us start school, we are encouraged, pushed, driven to achieve, to be better than the rest. Those who do not succeed are seen as inferior, and if they offer serious competition they often become scapegoats. Because our society still offers socially approved scapegoats, people can direct their hostility against them without criticism.

Sometimes prejudices are maintained because they offer some advantage. The minority group can provide an "excuse" for a person's own shortcomings.

Conformity is another factor that keeps prejudice alive. We are all conformists in one way or another. It is easier to go along with what everyone else is doing than to offer an alternative. In some instances it takes more courage than we possess to challenge an existing attitude. Numerous studies have shown that people who move to a new area quickly pick up its prejudicial attitudes if they didn't have them before.

In his book *White Attitudes toward Black People*, Angus Campbell also found that levels of prejudice varied according to where people lived. His research showed that people from New England and the Western states were least bigoted. The Middle Atlantic states had a higher level of bigotry, and the Midwest and South came out on top. Even when people moved from those areas, they tended to take their racial attitudes with them.

The size of the area in which people grew up also showed differences in attitudes. People from small rural areas tended to be less positive in their attitudes, and those from large cities more positive.

In general, people who support violence against blacks are distinguished by a low educational level. They usually have no association with a church and are dissatisfied with their community.

For both men and women, age is a significant factor in racial attitudes. Young people between the ages of 16 and 19 recognize discrimination and are more sympathetic than are older people.

Another major influence that keeps prejudice alive is the

stereotyping of ethnic groups in the media. Italians are traditionally cast as Mafia types, connected with crime and brutality. Asians are either computer whizzes or kung fu experts. Women too often are portrayed as either witches or bitches.

In entertainment, blacks have suffered perhaps the most severe stereotyping. During the 1920s and '30s the black man was often portrayed as a "Sambo" character, a buffoon with oversized lips and bulging eyes, looking and acting foolish for the entertainment of white folks. The characterization dated back to the days of slavery when blacks were expected to sing and dance, as well as work, for their white "masters."

Products ranging from postcards and children's books to ceramic figurines kept the "Sambo" image alive. It also kept alive the myth that blacks were inferior. That led to widely accepted negative labels for blacks such as "darkies," "coons," "pickaninnies," and "niggers."

Even though that image was largely destroyed during the civil rights movement, many people who grew up comfortable with it could never quite give it up.

By now you have probably come to the conclusion that the whole matter of prejudice is very complicated. You're right. It would be nice if it were limited to a few attitudes and a few problems. That would be a lot easier to deal with. But it isn't. In most cases, people are prejudiced because of all the factors we have discussed, not just one or two.

It is hoped that this information has given you a better sense of why your parents are prejudiced. They too are a product of all those influences, and often their attitudes are not based on conscious decisions. Sometimes it helps to accept certain behavior when you know that the motives behind it are not malicious. Then you can be upset with what the person does, not with the person.

What we have covered in this chapter, however, are not the only reasons people are prejudiced. It is a complex issue, and we shall look at some of the other reasons in the next two chapters.

CHAPTER 4

Were We Born This Way?

"Racism is a serious problem throughout the world. It divides society, makes people feel inferior, and destroys the meaning of equality to men."

That quotation is from an essay that won second place in "A World of Difference" essay contest in 1990. It was written by Julie Zucker, who was then a senior at South Garland High School, in Garland, Texas.

Her words reflect the reality of today, but racism is not a problem that just happened one day. It took a lot of history to get us where we are.

To fully understand the nature of prejudice and bigotry, we have to go back to the beginning of mankind. An attitude that is commonly called *tribal mentality* dates back to primitive society when clans developed. Clans had their own territories, and anything outside the group was viewed as a potential threat. Since little or nothing was known about an outside group, the natural inclination was to be afraid and set up defenses against possible attack.

The clans were characterized by fierce loyalty and protectiveness toward their own kind, which prompted them to acts that many of us would find difficult to understand. But the people of that time were concerned with survival, pure and simple. They had to provide food and shelter, keep the clan healthy and strong, and protect it from outside threat. If that meant attacking and killing anyone who came too close to the village, that is what they did.

With the necessity to protect the group, most of what those primitive people did kept the group turned inward and encouraged separateness. It laid the groundwork for the development of an attitude called *ethnocentrism*.

Simply defined, ethnocentrism means believing that one's own group is the center of everything. It is often characterized by feelings of superiority and loyalty to the group. Taken to extremes, it can lead to hatred and contempt for outsiders.

As people began to be civilized, one would expect things to have improved. But time and time again man reverted to some of the basic instincts of self-preservation and survival.

Sound a bit farfetched? Think about it. Even today, the conflicts that arise between people immediately create division. You can almost see the imaginary line drawn between two people or two groups with *us* on one side and *them* on the other. Each group is loyal to itself and aggressive to outsiders.

A perfect example is the conflict in the Broadway show and movie "West Side Story." Most of the time the Anglos and Puerto Ricans lived fairly peaceably in the neighborhood until someone from one group or the other crossed the line. The conflict erupted when an Anglo boy fell in love with a Puerto Rican girl, an act that crossed the line in a big way.

Tempers flared on all sides as right and wrong were debated, and only a few people thought it was a mistake to have a street war over the incident. The majority believed they had to protect the integrity of their group. The few dissenters were overruled. So the fight was on, and the rival groups battled it out. In the end nothing was resolved. People were hurt or killed, but nothing changed the attitudes that motivated the problem in the first place.

If you have seen "West Side Story," perhaps you got the message of how foolish some of our human instincts are. Maybe you have even vowed never to be like that. Then somebody starts making fun of the group you belong to, and your defenses flare. You have this hot flush of anger, and you're ready to do anything to preserve your group.

Perhaps if mankind had not started out with the instinct of protectiveness and survival and carried it throughout history, we could be different. But as it is, centuries of conditioning have made us what we are. Change is not going to come swiftly or easily.

Looking back on history, we can understand how primitive societies formed their attitudes toward outsiders, but it becomes harder to understand as civilization expanded. Once people came to have more contact with others who did not harm them, wouldn't their attitudes change?

Part of the reason things did not change was that as communities, countries, and nations evolved, separateness evolved with them. People within a common culture were divided by class or *caste*, with roles determined by their place in that society. In ancient Greece, for example, only landowners could be citizens and enjoy the benefits of

Greek culture. Slaves provided labor but shared in none of the benefits or dignity given to the citizen.

As feudalism developed, people were still divided into classes. Merchants, commoners, and slaves were at the bottom and were expected to provide for the needs of the knights, lords, and monarch. Merchants were treated with a bit more respect than slaves or commoners, but all three groups were denied the benefits and dignity shared by royalty.

This division of people into groups seldom had anything to do with race or color, however. According to Ashley Montagu, a noted anthropologist, people were persecuted in early civilizations because of religious, political, cultural, or class differences. Racial considerations became a factor only later.

During the fifteenth and sixteenth centuries, exploration took people farther from the continent of Europe. Explorers who traveled to Africa, the Far East, and America returned home with stories about the "savages" they had encountered. As they described strange customs and life-styles so alien to "civilized Europe," it was natural for the light-skinned Europeans to see these people as "subhuman."

That was probably the beginning of the modern theory of white supremacy. It also continued to promote ethnocentrism, which was often endorsed by religion. Missionaries traveled to those "backward" places believing that they had a divine duty to civilize the savages. The customs, beliefs, and possible dignity of the "savages" were seldom considered. The missionaries believed they were right, which was easily translated into "superior."

Through the early part of the twentieth century, the attitude of white supremacy was justified by theories based on mistaken scientific studies. Some scientists believed that light-skinned people were higher on the evolutionary ladder, and darker-skinned races were classified as the link closest to animals.

Because those ideas were presented by scientists, they were widely accepted as fact. The average person in the 1800s and early 1900s did not have the advantage of education or the luxury of critical thinking as you do today. Like the primitive societies, they were too concerned with matters of survival to question what "experts" told them.

Also, results of intelligence testing seemed to support the scientific theories. Certain races, mainly blacks, scored lower on IQ tests, and it was reasoned that they did so because they were biologically inferior. Many racist groups, especially the Ku Klux Klan, used that information and reasoning to justify their purpose.

But, as we shall see in Chapter 6 on stereotyping, the tests results were wrong. There is absolutely no scientific proof than any race is superior or inferior to another.

One of the reasons racism has been tolerated throughout history is the belief in social class as a birthright. Racists see humanity as divided into inferior and superior races distinguished by color. Positions of leadership in civilized lands have always been reserved primarily for whites. The royalty that ruled much of Europe for centuries was white, and the social attitude of white superiority sailed across the ocean with our ancestors.

The Europeans who settled in America considered themselves the "civilized" coming to a wilderness. Because the life-styles and cultures of the Indians were so different, the early settlers looked on the Indians as lesser beings. They did not meet the standards of education, religion, and social guidelines that determined acceptability, which reinforced the settlers' attitude of superiority.

When slaves were brought to the New World the

standard of superiority based on color became even more pronounced. People with dark skin, first the Indians and now the slaves, were seen as heathens. In the eyes of the Puritans nothing was worse than a heathen. To many it was barely one step up from the animals, so it is easy to see how such great divisions grew between groups.

The whole idea of slavery introduced other new aspects to the problems between the settlers and the "others." Most people were accustomed to a system in which servants worked for a certain period of time and then became free. It was a system that had existed for centuries in Europe.

Slaves, however, had no end to their contract. They didn't even have a contract. As possessions of their owners, they had no more rights than a horse or a donkey and often were not even thought of in human terms. Some owners treated their slaves decently—the same ones who treated their livestock decently. But many others were incredibly cruel, beating the slaves, overworking them, and simply replacing them when they died.

Books have been written discussing the impact of slavery on our society and racial attitudes. It is enough here to recognize two main points: first, the attitude of superiority and how it was formed, and second, the basic lack of dignity afforded blacks because of slavery.

Most of us could not even imagine how it must feel to be treated as a thing instead of a person, or how hard it is to rise above that treatment. It is that lack of dignity that has played a significant role in the problem between black and white even to this day.

Probably a main reason we tend to promote separateness even though we no longer need it for survival is the sense of comfort we find in the group we belong to.

Unfortunately, the formation of "in" groups always leads to the formation of "out" groups.

The boundaries between these two groups are marked by three major characteristics:

Proximity.   Things close together are more likely to be seen as parts of the same group.

For centuries, proximity was limited in scope. We lived in separate neighborhoods and went to separate schools. Cities, states, and countries were very exclusive in the sense of preserving themselves as separate entities.

Similarity.   Similar things are more likely to be seen as parts of the same group.

That is why we automatically decide that a guy with glasses and a calculus text in his hand is probably a nerd. That's how all nerds look, isn't it?

The way we dress is often a badge of identification, and it is not wrong. It helps us feel part of the group. But when others misinterpret or misuse the badge, it can lead to incorrect stereotypes. That guy with glasses might not be a nerd at all.

Common Fate.   Things that move together toward the same goal are more likely to be perceived as parts of the same organization.

It is much like the different social groups that form at school. You tend to be more comfortable around kids with whom you share a common interest than trying to get in with another group entirely. Most of the time you probably don't even think about it; you do it automatically.

Perhaps you thought that the importance of being part of a group was something we all outgrew. Unfortunately, we don't. We may learn to maneuver toward the most important group in less obvious ways. But the truth is, we all tend to *group* ourselves and to cling to the group with which we are most familiar and comfortable.

An adult social affair adjusts itself to that reality just as a teenage party does. The people who know each other from work cluster together. The neighbors seek each other out. Old college friends find each other and share memories. It takes a conscious effort for most people to break away from the known group and approach the unknown. Most of the time it is not done. It is simply easier to stay with the group, and our reasons often have little to do with the other groups. It is our own personal safety net that we use to help us feel secure and comfortable.

In the purely social sense, grouping is not necessarily prejudiced or racist. It is, however, part of the reason we carry the tendency to group over to the way we interact on a broader level. Like the people of early civilization, we still tend to view the unknown with a twinge of fear and vulnerability.

"Maybe I should go talk to those people across the room . . . Nah. It's easier to stay where I am."

"Maybe I should get to know some people from another culture . . . find out more about them . . . Nah. It's easier to stay where I am."

Sometimes separateness can be caused by cultural pride. That is not always prejudicial in nature. It is more a sense of pride in what it means to be Mexican, Indian, Spanish, Asian, or a member of any other ethnic group. Each group has characteristics that make it special, and most members feel good about that.

The danger of cultural pride is when it gets out of control. Pride is good for building confidence and self-esteem, but it can be a negative force when it leads to attitudes of superiority. Many people support their prejudicial attitudes with that superiority, and it is dangerous no matter what the ethnic group.

Now that we have outlined the historical and sociological development of prejudice, it is important to point out that most people do not consciously react from that. If your parents are prejudiced, they are not aware of all the history that led to their attitudes. Prejudice has become a belief based on the history, but if you asked your parents about it, they probably couldn't explain it.

In fact, most prejudiced people do not think too deeply about their attitudes or how they got them. Sometimes they can recall an influence from their parents or relatives, but even that is minimal. The propagation of bigotry is rarely an organized teaching campaign. With a few exceptions, parents do not deliberately teach their children to hate members of another ethnic group. However, they do communicate the prevailing attitude in subtle, often unconscious, ways.

What is important for now and for the future is for you to understand all that has gone before. The separateness we have lived with is no longer valid in today's world of global dimensions. People of all ethnic backgrounds must learn to live together in harmony, and understanding where we have been can help us know how to get where we need to go.

Chandra Thornton, whose essay won first place in "A World of Difference," has a vision of a new kind of history. "My solution [to the problem of racism] is not to become adjusted to prejudice, but to be a positive example for my race and a credit to my community and, perhaps, to the world. I, too, have a dream—a dream of teachers having to explain to a class what the world was like before prejudice was eliminated, and to think I had some part in solving this problem. If everyone everywhere were to take a part, soon it would be a whole—the whole world. In conclusion, the only time a man should look down on another is when they are reaching down to pick him up."

Chandra was a senior at Trimble Tech High School in Fort Worth when she wrote her essay. In it she issues a challenge to all of us to do our part to make a difference. If we expand our awareness and appreciation of people we used to think of as "outsiders," maybe we'll find that we share a common fate with all people.

CHAPTER 5

Don't Judge a Book by Its Cover

You have heard all the terms before: "He's a bigot." "That was an act of racism." "She is prejudiced." Do they all mean the same thing? Not necessarily. Even though the words are related and are often used interchangeably, the subtle differences are worth noting.

In the dictionary, bigotry is defined as "a strong conviction or prejudice in matters of religion, race, or politics, with an intolerance of those who feel differently." Prejudice means "a hostile or negative attitude toward a distinguishable group based on generalizations taken from faulty or incomplete information." Racism is defined as "the belief that certain races, especially one's own, are inherently superior; discriminatory behavior or practices based on this view."

While the words have subtle differences in meaning, they all feed from each other. Prejudice can lead to bigotry, which often leads to stereotypes and ends up in discrimination. For example, because of the tensions in the

Middle East you might make a prejudgment that all Arabs or Iranians are terrorists. You carry that prejudgment with you the next time you go to a convenience store. Even though the Iranian clerk is very nice to you, you still joke with your friends about the "ragheads" and agree that they should all be shipped back. In effect, you have stereotyped that clerk.

On a more serious level, many adults feed their prejudice with stronger stereotypes. They are also in a position to discriminate in more important areas such as jobs, education, and housing. Discrimination can take many forms. It may mean avoiding certain people, excluding them, or even resorting to physical abuse.

Prejudice is not limited to racial issues. People are discriminated against for many other reasons. Going back to the definition, the key phrase is, "a negative attitude toward a distinguishable group." There are all kinds of distinguishable groups; anything that makes a person different can put him in that classification. Unfortunately, we all too often make that difference a reason to limit that person.

A good example is women's issues. We know that women have long been discriminated against, especially in the workplace. Studies show that they earn less money than their male counterparts, and their career advancement is often slower.

Some people have maintained that women are less capable in the world of business, not logical enough or tough enough. It is also argued that women should not be allowed on jobs requiring physical strength or ability. Then too, some people still believe that woman's place is in the home. It is a combination of all those attitudes that affects the way women are treated in the workplace.

Through the work of organizations such as the National

Organization for Women (NOW), some progress has been made in eliminating discrimination against women. Legislation on state and federal levels has also made a difference in the past twenty years. Slowly, the old attitudes have been giving way to more freedom of choice for women, but there is still much to be done.

Another form of discrimination is based on age. By law, potential employees may not be passed over because they are fifty or older, but it happens. Recruiters and employment consultants see it all the time. Now they advise clients not to include their birthdate on résumés to avoid being turned down before they even get a chance for an interview.

Mandatory retirement is another form of age discrimination. In essence, being forced to retire tells a person that he or she is no longer useful to society. The effects of that attitude can be devastating to a growing segment of our society. As one man who was forced into retirement puts it, "Not being needed is the worst feeling in the world."

Here again, the issue revolves around choice. When a person's right to make a free-will choice is taken away, it is discrimination.

Sex and age discrimination probably affect the greatest number of people, but there are other areas as well. Disabled people experience it, and so do people who are overweight. They face it not only in the workplace but also socially.

To cover all the forms of discrimination adequately would take volumes. For our purpose, it is enough to know that they exist and are just as harmful as racial discrimination. The rest of the book focuses on racial issues because they cause the greatest conflict between teens and their parents.

PREJUDICE

Some prejudice is merely a matter of blind conformity. We don't know any better, so we go along with the crowd.

Other forms of prejudice have greater meaning for the holder. For instance, the white supremacy groups we shall look at later in this chapter have a self-serving purpose for their prejudice. Misguided as it is, their goal is to preserve the dominance of the "chosen group."

A bigot is defined as "A person who is stubbornly and unreasonably attached to an opinion or belief." *Stubborn* and *unreasonable* are key words in the whole problem of bigotry.

Prejudiced people tend to be inflexible. They are unable really to listen to information contrary to their attitudes, so you cannot reason with them. They brush off every point you try to make, almost as if saying, "Don't bother me with facts. My mind is made up and I'm right."

Prejudice is a matter of attitude and belief. Usually, the attitude is based on the belief. For example, "I don't trust Jews (attitude) because they cheat people (belief)."

For most people the belief is easy to challenge and can often be changed. A person who believes that Jews cheat others only needs the opportunity to do business with honest Jews to discover that his belief is in error. The belief can then be changed. Changing attitudes, as we shall learn later, is much more difficult.

The many levels of prejudice range from extreme to mild. People on the extreme side tend to be more vocal about their opinions and are more openly dangerous than mildly prejudiced people. Some have banded together in racist organizations such as the Ku Klux Klan, the Aryan Nation, the Arm of the Lord, the Christian Patriots Defense League, and the White Americans Resistance.

Most of these groups share several characteristics. Although primarily white supremacy groups, they do not limit their bigotry to blacks. Many of them are anti-Jew, anti-Oriental, and anti-anyone who does not agree with them.

These groups pose a double threat to racial harmony. Not only do they promote violence, they also offer subtle reinforcement to the negative stereotyping and myths associated with the object of their bigotry. By playing on people's fears and dissatisfactions, hate groups perpetuate the problems that continue to separate us. Sometimes they even persuade nonviolent people to support violence in an effort to maintain what they consider the rightful order of things.

Some of these groups are *paramilitary* in style and training, and there is nothing subtle about their actions. Over the years many acts of violence have been associated with them, including vandalism, harassment, assault, and even murder.

- In 1981 Klansmen harassed Vietnamese fishermen in Galveston Bay, Texas, burning their boats and homes.
- In 1981 Klansmen in Mobile, Alabama, beat, strangled, and hanged a young black man who was walking to the store.
- In 1989 Confederate Skinheads vandalized a Jewish synagogue in Dallas.
- In 1983 Klansmen bombed the Montgomery, Alabama, offices of the Southern Poverty Law Center in an attempt to destroy evidence of illegal Klan acts.
- In 1987 Klan members jeered, shouted insults, and threw bottles and rocks at peaceful civil rights

marchers in Forsyth County, Georgia, injuring several marchers.

- In 1989 Skinheads attacked an Ethiopian man in Oregon and beat him to death.

It is only recently that groups such as the KKK have been held accountable for their actions, although it is hard to figure out why. If the groups have committed crimes, why haven't more of them been tried, convicted, and punished?

To find an answer, we have to look back at history. Since the KKK is the oldest racist group in the United States, understanding how it developed over the years may help us understand the mentality of all the groups.

Interestingly, the KKK was formed by a small group of Confederate veterans almost as a joke at the end of the Civil War. With nothing to do, they were bored and restless and decided it would be fun to ride to neighboring homes at night with surprise visits.

Those original Klansmen intended no harm. Their little "club" had no sinister purpose. The costumes were part of the spirit of fun, and they only engaged in a few harmless pranks.

In his book *The Ku Klux Klan, America's Recurring Nightmare*, Fred Cook writes that those early members had no idea that their innocent beginning would lead to hatred and violence. It was when reports of unknown ghostly riders began to sweep the countryside that the club took on a whole new meaning.

As the South struggled with Reconstruction after the Civil War, other people began to see the Klan as a way to fight the changes that were taking place. Many Southerners in influential positions still felt strongly about preserving the way of life they had fought to maintain. Now here was the Klan, which could be used as a weapon against the influence of the disruptive outsiders.

The political leadership had no control in most Southern states during that difficult time. It was a free-for-all, with confrontations between the Carpetbaggers and their militia, federal troops, and an ever-growing Klan membership. Unfortunately, some members on all sides were often poor and uneducated, considered by some to be human riffraff. There was little or no organization behind the militia or the Klan, and their confrontations often resembled barroom brawls.

In 1876, President Rutherford B. Hayes removed the federal troops from the South, and the era of Reconstruction officially came to an end. Life for most people returned to normal, and the Klan all but disappeared for some time.

The period of racial tranquility was short-lived, however. By 1890, white politicians were using black voters as pawns in their maneuvering for power. As the various parties struggled to control leadership positions, antagonism mounted, and blacks began to object to being so used. The Klan was reborn to help the white leaders keep the blacks in line.

Until the early 1900s, racial bigotry had been pretty well confined to the South, but it was soon to be introduced across the nation. In 1915 a Southern minister, Thomas Dixon, Jr., wrote a book that became a major motion picture, "The Birth of a Nation." Glorifying the actions of Klansmen who fought the "wild black men" who were ravaging innocent Southern women, the film incited intense racial prejudice. The Klan was introduced to the nation as a band of heroes, and they reached a level close to respectability.

With the popularity of the film, a wave of bigotry swept the nation, but it was no longer focused only on blacks. Jews, Catholics, and immigrants became objects of hatred and harassment. When the Klan put on their robes and mounted their horses again, they proclaimed themselves the only one hundred percent Americans.

Although racism was no longer just a regional concern, Klan activity was still pretty much confined to the Southern states. Despite the general acceptance of the Klan, people in other areas were not clamoring to join. It had been reorganized under the leadership of William Simmons, a former minister, and it still rode in secret.

Texas and Louisiana particularly became hotbeds of violence. The Klan turned into a vigilante organization, taking upon itself the responsibility for policing society against those elements they saw as evil. Because of its "noble cause" of keeping America pure for Americans, the Klan could commit the most atrocious acts under the guise of high principle.

During the height of the civil rights movement in the late 1950s and early '60s, Klan membership and activity accelerated in efforts to maintain the status quo. Its attitude was that blacks are second-class citizens, and we can all live in harmony as long as they stay in their place.

Every civil rights effort fueled the antagonism between black and white, and extreme violence was commonplace. White politicians banded together, using their influence to protect the Klan and its right to keep blacks in their place. They could not openly support the Klan's criminal activities, but more often than not they looked the other way.

It was not until the mid-1960s, when the Klan launched a massive campaign of violence and terror against civil rights workers, that legal action began to impact the organization. Its activities became horrible front-page headlines across the nation, and the Klan found itself less able to get away with the atrocities members were committing.

The public attitude turned so negative that it still amazes some people that the Klan continues to exist. William P. Sullivan, Assistant Director of the Federal Bureau of Investigation during the '60s, has been quoted as saying he viewed Klansmen "like hoodlums" when he was a boy and adding, "I never learned anything about them to cause me to change my opinion."

If the Klan is widely recognized as disruptive and dangerous, why does it continue to exist? Why do people still support it?

Part of the answer lies in group dynamics. To promote self-esteem within groups and preserve a conviction that "We are right," there is often powerful pressure to conform. Individually, a KKK member may question some of the beliefs and actions of the group, but at a meeting he would never dare voice those objections.

For groups to maintain themselves, they need *cohesiveness*, *consensus*, and *insulation*. Their loyalty to the group holds them together (cohesiveness). Their need to conform within the group leads to common agreement (consensus). And that consensus insulates them against other opinions or ideas.

Some sociologists call this phenomenon *group think*. It is part of the dynamics of almost every group, although the degree of involvement varies as do the consequences. Group think also explains why there is strength in numbers and why it is so difficult to take an unpopular stand.

You may, for example, have the courage to tell your best friend that you don't think it is right to bar a student with AIDS from your school. If, however, you serve on the student council and it supports discrimination, it will be much harder to speak up.

Perhaps your parents are active members of the PTA or the school board, and they, too, are against admitting that student. The more your acceptance by these groups is threatened by your opinion, the more you will feel a need to conform in order to avoid the risk of ridicule and alienation.

Another reason people accept the status quo of bigotry, whether in an organized group or not, is that they are so accustomed to it. They see it as the way things are and believe it is accepted by everyone else. This is a subtle form of denial: "What problem? We don't have a problem."

Through denial, many people become apathetic about the issue. They blind themselves to possible injustice because it might upset the even balance of their lives. If there is a problem, they might have to do something about it. It's easier to keep pretending everything is okay.

That apathy on the part of the general public has been a major factor in allowing the continued existence of white supremacy groups.

In more recent history, some of the focus of the new Klan has been to recruit high school students into the Klan Youth Corps. Literature is distributed outside of schools calling on white students to "fight for white power" by joining.

The Klan blames the increased violence in schools on certain ethnic groups and use it as a rationale for their prejudice. It is the same rationale that has been used throughout history, and until people know better they are willing to accept it.

THE HARMFUL EFFECTS OF RACISM

There are several degrees of racism, and the harmful effects vary. The least harmful level is merely talking about one's attitudes. A bigot may trade racist jokes or remarks with friends, but he never goes any further. Most of the time he isn't even aware that he is prejudiced.

Other than offending people, this level of bigotry has no serious consequences to others. It does, however, support the negative stereotypes and limit the person's ability to see past them.

At the next level the bigot avoids a certain group because of prejudicial attitudes. That perpetuates the prejudice because it deprives the person of the opportunity to learn anything different about the group. Knowing nothing different, he can justify his prejudice.

This level also promotes the idea of separateness. It is somewhat like a personal segregation policy: "We're all okay with you over there and me over here." "Separate but equal" is a doctrine that has never worked.

A third level of racism is discrimination, which carries prejudice into an active mode by excluding members of a group from employment, housing, education, or social activities.

Even though segregation is no longer legal, many influential people still promote it quietly. The harm it causes is not limited to missed opportunities. What it says to groups of people about their worthiness does great harm. Imagine what it would be like to be told constantly, "You're not as good as we are."

Still another level of bigotry is physical abuse. It requires an extreme degree of prejudice to provoke someone to violence against a person simply because of racial or cultural differences. But unfortunately, as history can attest, it has happened and continues to happen.

The highest level of a violent expression of prejudice is extermination. The Holocaust is the most vivid and poignant illustration, but examples from American history are no less tragic. The massacre of thousands of Native Americans and the death of countless blacks during the era of slavery are facts that none of us can be proud of.

Some people rationalize that their first- or second-level prejudice really is not harmful. They may say, "It doesn't hurt anybody for me to feel this way."

The harm, according to Gordon Allport in *The Nature of Prejudice*, is that everyone starts at the first level. Even Hitler did. But fueled with enough emotion, the progression to more dangerous levels can be swift.

Those first two levels are no less harmful to the object of the racist attitudes. One need not be physically assaulted to feel attacked by bigotry. What about the feeling of hostility that can be sensed when a black guy walks into a room full of whites—or when a white guy walks into a room full of blacks? Primarily, they promote separateness because we immediately regress to the ancient and inevitable "us against them."

That has happened a number of times to Karen, a young black professional woman. "Every time we go to a party we have to test the waters," Karen says. "And even when you feel you're safe, maybe you're not."

The safety Karen refers to is not physical safety, but sefety from racist remarks or comments. She recalls a Super Bowl party where she and her husband were the only blacks, and how offended she was when someone yelled, "Look at that nigger run!"

Karen also feels hurt, disappointed, and angry because there are certain places it's wiser not to go just because she's black. She has always wanted to go to the Bed and

Bath resorts in East Texas, but her husband reminds her how exclusive they are. She is resigned to his logic but not happy about it. "It's just not fair."

Most of you probably agree with Karen. Discrimination is not fair, but it continues to exist because people allow it. And the problem seems so enormous that you may wonder if there is really anything we can do about it.

Well, we can't start a crusade to wipe out the KKK single-handedly, but we can start a personal crusade to maintain fairness and equality in our own actions toward others. We can also be more sensitive to the other forms of discrimination we discussed at the beginning of this chapter. Awareness of the harm caused by any type of discrimination can be a first step toward finding a solution to the problems.

CHAPTER 6

The Union Label

STEREOTYPES

How many of the following statements have you heard?

- "Everyone knows that if you're Italian you probably have a Mafia connection."
- "Jews are so good in business because they're cheap."
- "Blacks have an attitude problem. They want everything handed to them without having to work for it."
- Japanese are really smart, but, boy, are they ever sneaky."

Those are common stereotypes assigned to certain groups based on generalizations. When people stereotype others, they assign identical characteristics to all persons in a group without regard for differences among individual members.

Stereotyping in the most general sense is not always an intentional act of abuse. Sometimes we all use simple

52

stereotypic terms in an effort to categorize things or people. Designating "the jock," "the cheerleader," "the brain," helps us define our views of people. We don't mean anything negative by it. Nor is it always seen as harmful by the group we are labeling. It is just a point of reference.

It is when stereotypes are used to belittle or intentionally insult that they become harmful. They are harmful to the person we are stereotyping as well as to ourselves. If we cling to the stereotype, we are denying ourselves the opportunity to get to know someone as an individual.

For example, if your best friend told you that the new guy at school was stuck up and unfriendly, you might never introduce yourself, fearing a snub. But if he really were not stuck up—just shy and overwhelmed by a new school— you would never get a chance to know him.

Not all stereotypes are negative; some can even be complimentary:

"Hispanics have close, loving families."
"Blacks are very loyal."
"Orientals are very smart."
"Irish are devoutly religious."

The basic problem with stereotyping, whether negative or positive, is that it limits our thoughts about a group to common generalizations. There is so much more to know about people who are different from us than those first thoughts that come to mind.

Stereotypes do not necessarily cause prejudice, but they can justify and reinforce it. Every act of violence or discrimination against a person because of ethnic background has been defended by an erroneous attitude. Hitler considered the Jews impure because of their heritage. To the KKK, blacks were no better than animals. To the U.S.

Cavalry the Indians were merely savage impediments to progress.

The more closely you look at historical events, the more you can see that much of the conflict between people is based on prejudicial attitudes. Often those attitudes are supported by the wide acceptance of stereotypes.

So perhaps a good question to ask ourselves is why we keep labeling people? Why don't we just throw out all the stereotypes?

Part of the reason we can't merely eliminate stereotyping is explained later in this chapter when we look at *categorizing*. But another factor that enters into the why of it all is that the origins of some common stereotypes arise from cultural or natural circumstances.

For instance, the stereotype of the overprotective Jewish mother who is obsessed with the status of her children comes from a bit of true cultural reality. Jewish people traditionally place great value on home, family, and children. For some it is the most important part of their lives, and they want to do well out of a sense of family pride and loyalty.

It is ironic that those same values are held by people in other groups without being a stereotype. But certain jokes and stories have assigned this stereotype exclusively to Jewish mothers.

That points up another angle of the problem of limiting. By perpetuating the myth that only Jewish mothers care so much about their children, we take a little something away from the rest of the mothers.

Another myth that grew into a stereotype is that blacks are physically stronger than whites. The attitude stems from a time when blacks were restricted to unskilled jobs that involved hard physical labor. It takes little deductive power to recognize that a person who works in construction will be stronger than one who operates a keyboard. But the stereotype leaves out all the whites, Hispanics, and others who work in construction. Couldn't they be as strong as the black guy who works with them?

Occasionally, the myth of strength is used to explain why so many blacks are involved in sports. It is said that they do better because they have strength and "natural prowess." It is true that black athletes dominate many sports, but not because of that myth. Primarily it is because for a long time sports gave young black people their only opportunity for success.

Perhaps one of the most damaging myths attached to blacks was that they were intellectually inferior to whites. For too many years this myth was supported by some members of the scientific community, who based their judgment on IQ tests.

Through the 1800s and into the mid-1900s it was widely believed that genetic characteristics caused blacks to score lower on IQ tests. No consideration was given to background, education, or experience.

In the book *The Race Bomb*, authors Paul R. Ehrlich and S. Shirley Feldman write, "The claim that blacks are genetically inferior to whites in intelligence is just plain silly. In our racist society, it is also just plain dangerous."

They go on to disprove the theory by explaining the fallacies of IQ test results as a true measure of intelligence. Because of different cultural and educational experiences, it is impossible to measure the intellectual ability of all people with the same handful of tests. It would be like judging the worthiness of animals based on physical superiority. Because an elephant can pull a larger load than a cat, is an elephant more important?

Here, again, a stereotype was built out of a small grain of truth. Yes, blacks did score lower on IQ tests, but the truth was distorted. It was then used to support prejudice and racism.

A stereotype often applied to Hispanics is that of the "macho" male who is strong and domineering. The history of Latin countries going back to ancient Rome set up the attitude that men are superior to women. Unfortunately, those attitudes are still part of many Spanish-speaking cultures. A man must prove that he is "macho" by bravery and sexual prowess.

Although this attitude is part of some Spanish cultures, we hardly need to say that many Hispanic men are kind, sensitive, and supportive of women. We also could find many men of other groups who fit the "macho" stereotype.

According to William B. Helmreich in *The Things They Say behind Your Back*, about one third of stereotypes can be said to have some truth to them. Even the false stereotypes often were based on some kernel of truth in the past. But that still does not mean that every member of the group conforms to the trait described.

The greatest service we can do to any individual of any group is to allow that person to be unique. Meet him or her as a person, not a label, and give him a chance to be known for who he is.

CATEGORIZING

At first glance, categorizing seems to be the same as stereotyping, but there are subtle differences worth noting. In fact, it is our natural impulse to categorize things that leads us to label people and things. It is a normal way of thinking.

As we go through life we are constantly receiving, processing, and evaluating information. Then we assign it certain slots in our memory to be retrieved later for reference. It is like having a built-in organizer that helps to keep things in order.

The use of categorizing as a normal function of mental housekeeping is not harmful or necessarily prejudicial. It is something we all do, and we use it in a variety of ways:

1. **For guiding our daily adjustments**. The way we react to events or situations is based on information gathered and stored at some point in the past. Again using the "organizer" analogy, consider your brain as a big filing cabinet with lots of folders for information. Your brain automatically retrieves bits of information to assist you in your reaction to situations.

For instance, what if a guy has been picking on you at school, and today you see him walking down the hall toward you? Your brain flashes the memory across your mind, and you immediately decide to turn around and go the other way. By your natural inclination to categorize, you have saved yourself from an awkward confrontation.

That is not to say that the guy would have picked on you this time. It was just a strong probability, and you had to make an intelligent judgment based on it.

2. **To identify a related object**. When we see a fairly large round object with white and black hexagons being kicked around in a field, we automatically think "soccer ball."

If we are behind a car that is weaving all over the road, we say to ourselves "drunken driver."

We use this method of identification in almost every facet of life. It helps us in what we do and how we react to situations.

Some categories are almost purely intellectual and can be called *concepts*. *Cat* is a concept based on what we know or have read about the species *Felis catus*. But how we feel about cats alters our perception of the concept. Maybe our grandmother told us that cats kill babies, so we dislike cats.

You can see the correlation here with our ethnic categories. No only do we know the concept of black, Jew, or Mexican, but we have a positive or negative feeling that goes along with the concept as it is stored in our mental organizer.

Not all categories are rational. Scientific laws are based on facts that have been proven over time, and some categorization of people is valid. It is true that most Orientals are small in stature, but it is not true that that somehow diminishes them as people.

The most important categories we have are our personal values, and those are often highly charged with emotion. We love certain things—ice cream, pizza, and the guy who sits next to us in English—and that prejudices us toward them. On the other hand, we hate other things—tests, curfews, and the guy who sits next to us in Algebra—and that prejudices us against them.

A key element in not allowing our natural inclination to categorize to become a negative in our thinking about groups of people is relying on facts. Instead of basing a judgment on unproven generalizations or a surge of feelings, we should take time to find out the truth.

In stereotyping, a distinction has to be made between the process, *categorizing*, and the product, *bigotry*. Walter Lippmann was one of the first sociologists to study stereotyping extensively, and he explained our normal use of it in categorizing. As early as 1922 he pointed out the difference between the normal use of labels to categorize and the use of stereotyping to promote bigotry.

HARMFUL EFFECTS OF STEREOTYPING

People tend to live up to expectations, both their own and those of others. If we treat people according to a preconceived idea, it can actually reinforce the negative stereotype. For example, white students who stereotype blacks as being overaggressive do not stand up for themselves when confronted by blacks. That often makes them attractive targets for those blacks who *are* aggressive. Thus the stereotype is justified.

Likewise, people who do not trust Jews treat them differently in business situations. Their manner may make the mistrust very evident, and the Jewish person reacts with wariness. That wariness can be misinterpreted as deceitfulness, and the stereotype lives on.

A more concrete example has been proven by statistical studies. Some ethnic groups do poorly in school as a direct result of prejudicial conditioning. Because of messages from outside, they have come to believe that they lack the ability to perform as well as others.

For instance, in a recent poll by the National Opinion Research Center, 30 percent of the blacks surveyed agreed with 56 percent of the whites who thought blacks tended to be "less intelligent" than whites.

Clarence Page, a columnist for the Chicago *Tribune*, found those results most distressing. In his column (January 18, 1991) he wrote, "That tells me how deeply the message of white superiority/black inferiority has become embedded in the public mind, particularly in a country where most blacks and whites still live quite separate lives and do much of their learning about each other secondhand."

Sometimes we are unaware of the profound effect on us

of what we hear from others. At other times the awareness is painful. Think back to a time when maybe a friend was mad at you and called you a loser. What happened to your confidence? Sure, you probably had some sharp insult to throw back to cover your hurt. But inside, a little piece of you shriveled up for a moment.

Now imagine you are part of an ethnic group that gets the message "loser" from all directions. It is hard to cling to a belief in your own self-worth when it is constantly bombarded by attitudes to the contrary.

Each time we support an attitude that demeans another person, we add our own blow to the destruction of that person. That sounds incredibly harsh, but it is true, and there is no way to rationalize ourselves out of it.

In the area of personal self-worth, blacks as a group have perhaps suffered more prejudice than any other. As a result, they not only have to overcome the prejudice but also overcome a certain personal hopelessness.

Frequently the prejudicial attacks and the hopelessness cause people to withdraw and turn inward. Sometimes they just live with the situation in resignation, doing nothing about the attacks or their own reaction to them.

At other times, however, anger begins to build and eventually spills out. Some experts label that reaction an *ego-defense*, and it can lead to militancy. It is ironic that some people's bigoted attitudes toward blacks are based on black militancy, and the militancy was created by the bigoted attitudes.

Stereotyping is not harmful only to the object. It can be harmful to the person doing the labeling. People often selectively look for and accept information that proves their beliefs. That, of course, is very self-limiting. How can we ever hope to "know any better" if we are not open to other information, even if it is contrary to what we believe?

When we stereotype, we also assume that everyone will act a certain way. A good example is what happened recently to Tony, a junior at Plano Senior High School in Plano, Texas. There was a controversy over Mark Twain's *Huckleberry Finn*, and some students and parents thought it should be removed from the required reading list because of language offensive to blacks.

At an open forum held at the school, Tony got up to speak in favor of the book. "It was kind of amusing in one respect," he says. "The minute I walked up to the microphone, I knew people were evaluating what I was going to say based on the color of my skin."

Many of the white students were surprised at the stand Tony took, and some of the black students accused him of selling out. But Tony doesn't see it that way at all. He supported the book because it portrays the evil and stupidity of racism so well. "The whole thing [racism] is just so ridiculous," he explains. "People get so hung up on words. And the words can mean different things to different people, depending on the circumstances."

As an example, Tony says that when he visits his grandparents in Arkansas, the neighborhood guys get together to play football. "If one guy gets mad at another, he'll call him a 'nigger'," Tony says. "And it's that same type of guys who protest a book like *Huck Finn*. Why is it okay for a black to call another black a 'nigger,' but it's not okay for whites?"

Tony's thought is to get rid of the words and labels entirely. "As long as we keep using them, they seem to have more validity."

The act of stereotyping also keeps some people from ever feeling anything in common with the object of the stereotype. That makes it easier to maintain separateness and can even depersonalize those others. If we cannot see them as real people, with the same hopes and dreams and feelings that we have, we can still see them as the "enemy."

Experts have also found a connection between stereotyping and people's ability to lose the restraint that usually keeps them from harming others. When the other person is seen as "bad" or "unworthy" it is easier to overcome the feelings of empathy, guilt, or anxiety that would keep most of us from violence.

That certainly would explain how some people are able to commit terrible acts against others and still lead ordinary lives. They simply fail to see the acts as bad.

Some people, like Tony, think the solution to the problem of stereotypes is simply to get rid of them. However, that is not only probably impossible to achieve, but is it really practical?

It is natural for us to describe ourselves in distinctive terms. What is obviously different about us is easier to notice and point out than what is the same.

According to Russell A. Jones in his contribution to the book *In the Eye of the Beholder*, it is also natural for us to use the same method in describing others. Doing that is not necessarily wrong or harmful. Often it is just a matter of quick reference.

What we must always be aware of, however, is what else we attribute to a person along with that distinctive term. Have we let go of all the unfounded presumptions that are associated with it?

We also have to be conscious of our own intent in using the distinctive term. Are we using it merely as a point of reference with no prejudice or malice?

Those are questions we all have to answer for ourselves. In finding our answers perhaps we can consider the following passage from a Letter to the Editor in the Dallas *Morning News* by Brian Barnette:

"An African-American student looked at a Confederate flag and saw only the enslavement of his ancestors.

"A Cherokee grandmother looked at the Statue of Liberty and saw only the horrors of the Trail of Tears.

"A conservative Senator looked at an artist's work and saw only the nudity of the subject portrayed.

"An upset father looked at a literary classic and saw only the words the author used.

"A weary shopper looked at a Nativity scene and saw only an attempt to lure customers into the mall.

"A social worker looked at a newborn child and saw only the specter of world overpopulation.

"Perhaps symbols, like beauty, lie in the eye of the beholder."

CHAPTER 7

The Brady Bunch

I t is common to hear the family referred to as "the backbone of society," and in terms of structure that is very true. Families are the first unit of society in which we learn to interact with other people. How family members relate to one another quite often determines how they will relate to other groups in society. It is like a ripple effect that flows over into work, school, church, and community.

It is in the family setting that we learn to handle conflicts, either effectively or ineffectively. We also learn how to set goals and accomplish them, along with a myriad other important lessons of life. In healthy family settings we learn how to be mature, responsible adults. We learn negotiating skills and effective problem-solving that enable us to handle ourselves better in an adult world.

In a dysfunctional family, however, the lessons are not as well learned. Individual family members miss that all-important experience to help them as adults. Very often, people whose family was unable to cope with their problems have to take a whole new set of problems into every area of their lives. Their effect on society can run from minimal to extreme. Frustrated, unhappy kids are more likely to become involved with drugs. Most felony offenders come from backgrounds of abuse and neglect. Employees with problems at home are absent from the job more often than others.

Those few examples illustrate the point. The recent breakdown of family structure in the United States has caused great concern among sociologists. So many of the problems we face in our society are linked to dysfunctional families, and it has to end.

Luckily, the mental health profession shares that concern. They are expanding services and agencies so that any family can find help in coping with their problems. Family counseling has become an integral part of many drug treatment programs. It is also an important part of support groups for abuse and other problems.

With this awareness and effort, perhaps we will see a reversal in the current trend.

"FATHER KNOWS BEST" OR "ROSEANNE"?

Families are as unique as people are. No two are alike, and every family falls somewhere on a scale between perfectly healthy and totally dysfunctional. It would be a mistake to assume that there are perfect families. Maybe there are in television, but not in real life.

"All real families have problems," says Dr. Jerry Weiss, a clinical psychologist who does family counseling in Dallas. "Healthy families just have better strategies for solving problems as they come up. Dysfunctional families don't have strategies. Or if they do, they are destructive strategies."

In describing a healthy family, Dr. Weiss draws a diagram:

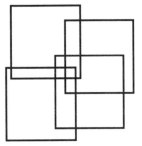

Each box represents a family member. Dr. Weiss explains that healthy family relationships have overlapping, yet clear, boundaries. Each family member recognizes and respects those boundaries, so each one is able to grow individually while growing as part of a unit.

Key elements of a healthy family relationship are respect, fun, nurturing, support, and unconditional love. Families that really care about each other are more accepting of each other's differences and do not withhold love or affection because of a disagreement. Perhaps that is why the bond of Jimmy Hudson's family was not broken, even though they disagreed so strongly about bigotry.

In the book *Resolving Family Conflicts: Everybody Wins*, Mendel Lieberman and Marion Hardie mention three other key ingredients of healthy family relationships:

1. I feel good about myself (self-esteem).
2. The other family members feel good about themselves.
3. We communicate in ways that enhance and strengthen each other's self-esteem.

These points make a good yardstick for measuring your own family relationship. If you turn the statements into questions and can answer yes to them, you probably have a pretty healthy family.

1. Do I feel good about myself?

If you have a lot of confidence in yourself, it is probably because you come from a nurturing family. They helped you to recognize your strengths and made you feel like an important part of the group. Without that kind of support, it is hard for people to grow up feeling good about themselves.

2. Do the other family members feel good about themselves?

If you answered yes to 1 you would almost have to answer this one yes as well. A family could hardly be nurturing and supportive of one another if one member were unhealthy. That is why Alcoholics Anonymous offers support groups for every member of the alcoholic's family. Like many other problems, it is not an individual matter. Everyone is affected, and everyone has to learn how to function on a healthy level.

3. Do we communicate in ways that enhance and strengthen our self-esteem?

In healthy families people support each other by recognizing and pointing out the good they see in each other. They try to find ways to make each individual feel important and needed. Also, they do not tear each other apart in arguments. During a confrontation they resist the temptation of name-calling and put-downs.

Just as there are no perfect families, there are no totally dysfunctional families. But, again, a growing number of families operate on some level of unhealthiness. For the purposes of this book, however, there is no need to go into details about how and why families are unhealthy, except as it pertains to problem-solving.

As Dr. Weiss explains, healthy and dysfunctional families have different approaches to dealing with problems. Healthy families use strategies that heal and strengthen, whereas dysfunctional families tend to use destructive strategies.

To illustrate that point, Dr. Weiss uses the example of a young woman who is divorced with one child. Everyone who is related to that woman is affected by the divorce. Parents, brothers and sisters, her child, and other extended family members are all touched in some way. How they all cope is a good indication of how healthy they are as individuals and as a family unit.

"A natural tendency," Dr. Weiss says, "especially for parents, is to want to help. They want to do as much as they can to ease the burden for the daughter. But healthy families won't take it to extremes. They won't smother the daughter by telling her what to do, when to do it, and how. They'll respect her maturity and allow her to make her own decisions, even if they think the decisions are wrong."

Dr. Weiss continues that healthy families do not waste time on negative thinking or talking. In a divorce situation it is natural to have anger, which often leads to criticism and blaming. "He was such a dirty rat." Or, "She was so selfish. She only wanted things her way."

Blaming and criticizing are among the most destructive things family members can do to each other. Dysfunctional families are often caught up in a vicious circle of criticism and blaming. It is all they know how to do when they try to cope, and they fail to realize that they are destroying everyone's self-esteem in the process.

Again using the example of the divorced young woman, Dr. Weiss says that a dysfunctional family not only blames but also can turn the woman into a victim. "This terrible thing happened to her, and now she is a poor lost soul." They smother her with pity until she may not be able to rise above it. She believes she *is* a poor lost soul and begins to act like one.

But unhealthy families do not have to stay that way. They can learn, either through counseling or experience, how to stop the destructive behavior.

CAN WE TALK?

Effective communication is a vital part of family relationships. We have to be able to let each other know what we think and how we feel on levels that are often uncomfortable. Many times, especially during a conflict, we talk about something that is totally irrelevant to what is really going on.

For example, perhaps you told your brother something in confidence. Then he told a friend, and it ended up being broadcast all over school. You come home and find him in your room going through your CDs. Normally, you borrow from each other all the time, but today you explode.

"Get out of my room, you dirty little sneak!"

"Hey, what's the problem?"

"This is *my* room and *my* stuff. And don't you ever touch it again."

"Well, la-de-da. Anything else from Your Highness?"

"I said, Get *out!*"

Bewildered, your brother leaves, and perhaps the two of you just glare at each other the rest of the day. Maybe, eventually, in a day or so, you talk it all out, or maybe you don't.

The communication problem is fairly evident in this little scene. You were not only angry with your brother for breaking the confidence, you were hurt and disappointed. Unfortunately, it is easier for most of us to express anger than it is to express hurt. Somehow hurt makes us feel more vulnerable.

There was no way you could say how much your brother hurt you. He might laugh, or worse, you might cry. So the real issue is hidden under the anger and sarcastic remarks.

Another fairly common example of miscommunication most of us can relate to is when Dad is storming around the house like a berserk "Rambo." If we're not too afraid, we may ask what's wrong, and the typical response is, "Nothing."

His answer should be reassuring if nothing were really wrong. But the gruffness of his voice and the expression on his face show that plenty is the matter. So there we are, wondering if we might be the cause of his obvious displeasure.

The first step to more effective communication is simply the ability to talk to each other. Not just chat about sports, weather, school, but really talk like people who care about each other. That brings us back to the first two elements of healthy families mentioned by Lieberman and Hardie.

When people feel good about themselves they have the confidence to be more honest in what they say to others. They also have the confidence to question the messages they receive. For instance, people with more personal confidence will question the Dad who snarls that nothing is wrong. They won't simply accept things at face value.

Misreading and misunderstanding the messages we get from one another is a major stumbling block to effective communication. To overcome it, we have to make a concentrated effort to improve our own skills.

1. **Try always to be totally honest in what we say**.

It is not productive to say what we think the other person wants to hear. Sometimes it is easier, but it serves no good purpose. For instance, maybe Dad asks if you are going to apply for admission to the University of Michigan. You don't really want to, but you know he wants you to. It is his alma mater, and he has talked about your going there as long as you can remember. Your instinct is to preserve peace at all costs, so you want to say, "Sure, I'm sending the application next week."

With that response, everybody loses. If you do go where Dad wants you to, you probably will not do well, and he'll be disappointed.

The best way to handle it is simply to tell Dad that you have nothing against the University of Michigan. You know it's a good school, and you know how loyal he feels to it. But you have wanted to go to UCLA for the last year.

2. **Make sure we understand the messages we get from other people**.

It is just as hard for people to be totally honest with us as it is for us to be honest with them. Take the example of the "Rambo" dad again. Maybe he was so angry and upset because he had just found out he might be laid off. That is pretty scary for someone who is responsible for so many people. The situation probably made him feel very vulnerable. However, expressing that vulnerability may be even scarier than the idea of being out of work. He is supposed to be a symbol of strength and security, and he is about to lose both.

Instead of running away in terror when Dad snarls at us, it would be better to tell him gently and lovingly that we know he acts like this only when something is bothering him. If he doesn't want to tell us right now, that's okay. But we want him to know that we care. When he is ready to talk about it, we would like to know what really is wrong.

3. **Don't listen with our answer running.**

That is a principle promoted by a number of programs for enriching family relationships, and it is an effective tool. When we really focus on the other person in the conversation, we can pick up on all the subtle messages beneath the words. If we are already planning our response while the other person is talking, we may miss the point entirely.

In the situation between you and your brother, he might have been able to help you address the problem if he had really listened instead of trading insults. Instead of putting up his defenses in the face of your anger, he could have asked what was the matter. When you came back with another order to get out of your room, he could have asked why. Why wasn't it okay to borrow your CDs that day when it was okay before? Eventually, you might have had the courage to tell him what was really bothering you, and the two of you could have resolved it.

This discussion by no means covers all the principles of good communications, but it is at least an overview of what is important. Just as the family is the foundation of society, communication is the foundation of effective problem-solving.

To achieve and maintain a good level of communication takes commitment by all family members. We cannot be evasive or self-seeking, and above all we must have the courage to be *real* to each other.

That does not mean we will never fall short of our goal or have problems. It just means that we care enough to make the effort, and that is one of the most important traits of strong families. A good family does not just happen. It develops over time. And when we make mistakes, we have to pick ourselves up and start over again.

Is it worth it? You bet. One man has said that if he had nothing else to show for his life, he was proud that he had good children who were now raising good families.

CHAPTER 8

The Brady Bunch
Goes to War

FAMILY CONFLICT

The simplest solution to family conflict would be not to have it any more. Wouldn't that be great? No more fights over dishes, curfew, your room, or who should take out the trash?

Unfortunately, it is not that simple. Conflict is a normal part of family life, and it can either pull a family together or push it apart. It depends on how each member deals with the problems causing the conflict.

Dr. Weiss has several suggestions for positive approaches to problem-solving:

Be aware of what the conflict really is about.

Do not accept things at face value. As we saw in Chapter 7, the problem is often not what is initially presented. We fight over what triggers our anger at the moment, but usually the major problem is something else.

Before you confront someone over a problem, think it through carefully. What are you upset about? Is it that your mother asked you to do the dishes when you came home from school and you blew up at her? Or is it because you got an unexpected assignment in history and you feel overwhelmed with stuff to do?

If you took a moment to think through your feelings and reactions, you could probably smooth things over with your mother. She might even sympathize with your predicament and offer to help you somehow.

Stick to the problem at hand.

Because of our natural tendency to defend ourselves, we often try to diffuse the conflict. We bring up unrelated subjects, or we lash out at the other person with what Dr. Weiss calls "old garbage." We've all thrown a bit of that around in our time—reminding our sister what a brat she was last November.

But that is counterproductive. What your sister did to you several months ago, or even last week, has no bearing on today's problem. If you cannot focus on the current problem and get it settled, it could fester for a long time. Then it too could become "old garbage" at a later date and interfere with the solution of a new problem.

Work for a win/win solution if at all possible.

To illustrate that point, Dr. Weiss uses the example of a family conflict over what movie to see. Johnny wants to see the latest kung fu film, and Mom is totally uninterested. At that point she has two choices. She can tell Johnny she won't go to that stupid movie, which means she wins and Johnny loses. Or she can offer a compromise that does not diminish Johnny or leave him out of the victory: she can offer to drop him at the theater next week to see the film he wants (nothing said about the quality of the film or his taste), but for tonight the majority of the family want to see something else. Since it is a family outing, what the majority want to see should rule. If Johnny will agree, they will top off the evening with a stop at the ice-cream store.

Two major things are accomplished with that approach. First, there is a satisfactory resolution. Second, the method of resolution teaches Johnny something about effective negotiating.

Dr. Weiss stresses the importance of good negotiating skills. We all negotiate in personal relationships, in work relationships, and other situations. Knowing how to do it without setting up further conflict by drawing battle lines makes things easier for everyone involved.

Other points from *Resolving Family Conflicts: Everybody Wins* support Dr. Weiss.

Make sure whose problem it is.

That is just as important as knowing *what* the problem is. If we assign responsibility for a problem to the wrong person, it may never get solved. A good example is when a mother gets totally frustrated with her son's misbehavior and threatens to tell Dad when he comes home. Maybe she is too tired to deal with it herself at the moment, but she really has made a big mistake. Whatever the problem is, it must be dealt with now. It is not right or fair to unload it on Dad. It is not even his problem, so why should he be involved?

How important is the issue?

Lots of jokes are made about the minor irritants that drive family members nuts—squeezing the toothpaste tube in the middle, taking the last cookie from the cookie jar, borrowing a sweater without asking . . . The list could go on forever.

Some people think those things are not worth fighting about, and maybe they wouldn't be if we could all learn to forget about them. Human nature being what it is, however, most of us do not forget them. Those irritating little things can turn into a litany of resentments that we recite in the middle of arguments.

Lieberman and Hardie believe it is better for families to confront the trivial issues so that they don't cloud up the more important ones.

How important is the relationship?

This point is related to the previous one. Sometimes we forget what we mean to each other when we are in the thick of an argument. It is difficult to separate our feelings about what has happened from our feelings in general.

When we are in the midst of a conflict with someone, our strongest feeling is usually anger. When we permit it, the anger rules, and we say some pretty hateful things to each other.

If the quality of brotherly love were measured only by what two brothers say to each other when they are really mad, it wouldn't register on any scale.

As we mature, we can learn to control the feelings and not act on them until we have cooled off a bit. That does not mean denying the feelings. We merely choose to postpone the confrontation until we are no longer blazing inside.

Whenever you have a disagreement with your parents you actually have two conflicts going on. One is whatever you are arguing about; the other is a conflict of emotions that you experience within. This internal conflict intensifies the closer you come to adulthood. You are asserting your independence, thinking more for yourself, and it seems in some ways that your parents still treat you like a baby.

Sound familiar? Every young person goes through it, but it certainly does not make you want to try to act mature. The more they treat you like a baby, the more you want to act like one. But it may surprise you to know that your parents are dealing with conflicting emotions as well.

Sometimes the hardest thing for parents to do is to let go of their children and allow them to become adults. The years between infancy and young adulthood pass so quickly that not every parent is aware of the need to treat you differently. Parents do not consciously decide to treat you like a four-year-old. They usually don't even realize that they should be letting go.

Some parents *are* aware but are afraid to let go. Perhaps they remember all the mistakes they made in their early independence, and they want to save you from that. They think if they continue making decisions for you, they can help you avoid some of the rough spots they encountered.

Whatever the reason, parents usually mean well when they try to control you. That does not make it right, but it does make it more understandable. With that understanding, you can diffuse some of your own anger when a confrontation arises and deal with it more reasonably. Keeping your anger under control may make it possible for your parents to do likewise.

FIND AN ENDING

The eventual resolution of problems is an important ingredient in a healthy family relationship. Problems have to be resolved, not pushed away in a corner. In *Making Peace with Your Parents*, Dr. Harold Bloomfield writes, "There are emotional wounds and even health burdens that we suffer from the unfinished business with our parents."

An example might be people with low self-esteem. As children and young adults they may have never felt acceptance by their parents. Somehow they just didn't measure up. They may go through life still seeking approval from others, because they never got it from their parents. That can be very damaging emotionally and can even lead to physical disorders.

Since the greatest difficulties in parent/child relationships seem to arise as we approach adulthood, it might be helpful to examine some ways parents and children can get along better as adults. Delores Curran, a well-known author and speaker on family matters, offers some suggestions.

At her workshops, she asks parents and teens to draw up a "wish list" of things they would like from the other person. The responses from parents about their teens include the following:

I wish . . . .

They would treat me with more respect.

They wouldn't get so defensive when I make a suggestion.

They wouldn't demean my beliefs.

They would at least listen to my opinion.

They would realize that we're human and forgive us for past hurts.

*   *   *

Surprisingly, the question drew similar responses from the
young people. Considering the correlation between the
answers, Ms. Curran concluded that parents and young-
adult children deal with the same issues in relating to each
other.

She also realized that a key issue revolves around
respect. Parents and young-adult children need to treat
each other with the same caring and consideration that
adults show one another.

On paper, that may seem fairly simple, but in practice it
presents quite a challenge. It asks everyone involved to be
more tolerant and accepting of each other. It asks us to take
responsibility for what we do to harm the relationship, not
to blame everything on the other person.

And again, it issues a challenge to your parents to
recognize your adulthood.

Ms. Curran believes that you can help your parents
come to that recognition by your behavior. She suggests
that you avoid reverting to childish reactions to your
parents' behavior.

If your parents are blind to the fact that you are
becoming an adult, don't let them hold you back in
childhood by what you do. Instead of an angry, childish
reaction to a disagreement, behave like the adult you want
to be. The more they see you acting like an adult, the
harder it will be for them to deny your growth.

Chris, a high school student, says that his parents have
been pretty good about treating him and his older brother
and sister like adults. Having mutual respect and consideration is an important part of how they operate as a
family. "Sure, we still get into arguments over things," he
says. "But we don't cross any bounds."

Chris can't explain exactly what he means by that, but it

has to do with respect. It is important to respect the other person as an individual as well as to respect his or her thoughts and feelings. "When I tell them how I feel about what we're discussing, they take that into consideration in what is decided," he says.

On the subject of "letting go," Chris's mother, Laura, says it has been easier with her sons. Her daughter is the eldest child, and Laura says, "As parents we tend to cling to the oldest ones longer. We get a little more flexible with the younger ones."

Part of the reason for that is that parents are generally more relaxed with the younger kids. They have had some experience and come to realize what works and what doesn't.

One of the things that works for Chris's family is common courtesy. "I always leave notes for the boys to let them know where I'm going to be," Laura says. "And if I find I'm going to be late, I call."

That may seem like a trivial thing, but it is part of acting like and being treated like an adult. By letting Chris know where she is, Laura says that he is important enough for her to take the time and trouble. That in turn makes Chris want to be more responsible about leaving messages as to where he is and when he will be home.

Another family habit is not making individual plans without consulting the family calendar. Like most families they are all busy with a variety of activities, and they often have to juggle schedules and transportation. Giving careful consideration to each person's needs in this juggling act reinforces his or her importance in the family.

From that kind of foundation, you can carry mutual respect into confrontations.

Chris says that he frequently gets mad at his mom and dad but he never puts them down. "I may say things like,

'You're not being fair.' But I never say things like, 'You're a rotten parent.'"

Laura says that she and her husband also try to maintain respect during a conflict. To illustrate, she relates an incident involving Chris's older brother, who had failed two subjects. "I spent several days being out of sorts with him," Laura said. "Every time I saw him I would get mad all over again. I was trying to find the best way to talk to him about it, and I finally realized that I just had to let him know how mad I was.

"But I also had to let him know that I wasn't just mad because he was failing. His failing had nothing to do with me. I was concerned about what he was doing to himself and how that would affect his future.

"I also wanted to know if something else was going on, something that might be bothering him that made him suddenly seem to scuttle himself that way."

Laura is quick to point out that they are anything but a perfect family, and Chris nods in agreement. They both agree that it takes a concentrated awareness to keep things good between family members. "But if everyone tries, it doesn't take a lot of effort," Chris says. "You just have to be open and honest."

WHEN THE BELL RINGS FOR ROUND ONE

No matter how good a family is at all the techniques of effective relationships, sometimes you still cannot avoid a fight over an issue. And having to fight is not always unhealthy. Utilizing certain principles of effective fighting can actually lead to growth in other areas of the relationship.

Commitment and genuineness. Each person should be committed to resolving the problem constructively. That means sticking to the point of the fight and not getting carried away by anger and frustration. It also means not holding back when it comes to deep feelings about the subject. We have to be honest in our responses while still being concerned about the other person's feelings. If we care only about ourselves, we are more apt to set up a win/lose situation than a win/win resolution.

Responsibility. We are responsible for our feelings, and it's not fair to blame others for them. To do that makes them "wrong" and us "right," setting up immediate barriers to resolution.

If we are angry because our best friend forgot to call us when she said she would, we can tell her how we feel without saying she was wrong. Instead of saying, "You make me so mad," we can say, "I'm really upset that you didn't call." In that way our friend need not be on the defensive, which would make her more resistant to any attempt to solve the problem.

Willingness to compromise. Stubbornly clinging to our own wants and needs closes down avenues of resolution. Willingness to make concessions not only opens the way to a solution but also eases tensions. Both parties in a conflict can relax a little when there is a genuine desire to find an equitable resolution.

Respect. There's that word again. The reason it keeps coming up is that respect is such an integral part of all aspects of relationships. It is also very often the principle that is forgotten first in a fight. We are angry and we want to lash out at the other person. Name-calling and "garbage dumping" are mainstays of most fights, and they are the most destructive. They undermine our ability to utilize the other principles of fair fighting. Who wants to compromise with the brother who calls us a dirtbag every time we argue?

One final point is to remember that none of us is perfect. Even though we know all these principles and are willing to use them, we won't always succeed. When we fail, we cannot let the failure keep us from trying again. Sometimes growth in a relationship can only be measured by how often we are willing to try again, not how often we succeed.

REAPING THE REWARDS

The most important benefits of a good family life are often not easy to measure in concrete terms. They go much deeper than what kind of house you live in or how new the family car is. Those things can be nice, of course, but the personal benefits of confidence, assurance, self-esteem, and integrity will be much more important in the years to come.

How well your family experience has prepared you in these areas can be determined by your answers to the following questions:

1. Do you feel free of the expectations of your parents?

That does not mean you are free of responsibility or family obligations. You still have to abide by the rules and contribute to the general family welfare, but you should be pursuing interests and goals that are your own. Do you play football because you enjoy the sport, or because Dad was a star quarterback? Are you planning to go to law school because you have a genuine interest in justice or because Mom thinks you would be a great lawyer?

2. Can you make a mistake without excessive self-criticism?

To be an emotionally healthy adult, you should have a clear view of yourself, recognizing your good and bad points. We are all imperfect, and we are all going to make mistakes. Rebounding and learning from our mistakes helps us in the maturing process. The only thing terrible about a mistake is if we make the same one over and over again. A mistake is often a one-time error in judgment; a problem is a mistake that repeats itself.

For instance, a friend asks you to go to a club or bar with her, using a fake ID. If you don't go, she'll go anyway, and you don't want her to go by herself; something awful could happen to her. So you convince yourself that it's better for you to go along. The guy at the door spots the fake IDs and decides to scare you. He threatens to call the cops, or at least call your parents. You plead with him until he finally agrees not to call if you go home and never try this again.

So what can you learn from a situation like that? Get better IDs? Well, that depends on whether you want to create a problem for yourself.

Perhaps the better lesson is to realize that no amount of rationalization can justify doing something wrong or unlawful. And even though you did it, that does not make you a bad person. You just made a mistake.

If you have grown up in a nurturing family, you have learned not to beat yourself up over your mistakes. If you have not had that advantage and are unnecessarily critical of yourself, you may want to get some help. You need to find a way to acknowledge your mistakes without losing self-respect and confidence.

4. Do you enjoy being responsible for the quality of your life?

That may seem misleading at first, since your parents probably still provide for your needs. But the question refers to the emotional quality of your life. Your happiness, your confidence, your success depend solely on you. No one else is responsible for how you feel, what you think, or what you do.

At this point you should have a pretty good idea of how strong your relationship is with your parents. Maybe you have even picked up a few tips to improve it. But the important thing about the last two chapters was to help you decide whether you can confront your parents about their bigotry. Since every situation is unique, you are the only one who can decide.

CHAPTER 9

Breaking the Cycle

Despite the many advances in race relations since the civil rights movement, some negative attitudes remain. Writer Joel Dreyfuss found that out when he polled the readers of *Black Enterprise* magazine for a 1980 feature story on racism. Ninety-six percent of the readers who responded believed that "whites harbor some form of racism toward blacks." Seventy-eight percent admitted to "some negative feelings toward whites."

From those responses, it is obvious that in many ways nothing has changed. We are still lining up on opposite sides of an imaginary line like grade-school bullies. Does that mean we just quit trying?

No!

Young people today are part of a new generation that can be of tremendous influence on racial harmony. You, more than any generation before you, have the advantage of being able to see our world whole instead of in segments. With so much of the world interdependent in business and economics, survival can no longer be exclusive to certain groups.

Knowing that and acting on it are two different things,

however. It is so much easier to go along with what we have learned in growing up. That is why so many people just accept things as they have always been.

James understands that attitudes are passed on from generation to generation. He knows that his parents think pretty much the way his grandparents did, but he does not want to continue the legacy.

"I always hated it when Dad made jokes or said things about blacks," he says. "Then when I got a little older, I found myself saying some of the same things. One day I realized I might turn into my father. Some of the things I was saying . . . it was like . . . good grief, that's my father speaking."

The realization made James really uncomfortable, and now he is beginning to watch what he says. "When I'm with Asian or Hispanic friends, I stop and think before I open my mouth. I also apologize when I do say something offensive."

The problems we all have to deal with about prejudice will not go away by themselves. It takes a certain amount of commitment and effort. That is what Earl Simpkins and Terry Pierce realized when they started a new organization at Plano Senior High in the spring of 1990. Called the Ethnic Club, it has three main purposes:

1. Enhance relations and conditions for all students at Plano Senior High.
2. Educate students about different cultures.
3. Work with administration in the event of racial tensions.

The club also formed an executive panel to meet regularly with the principal, teachers, and parents to discuss issues of ethnic concern. In the controversy over

Huckleberry Finn that was mentioned in Chapter 6 the Ethnic Club was a highly visible presence. Their input was part of the final resolution to have the book available but no longer on the required reading list.

Members of the Ethnic Club recommended that the book be reserved for upper high school classes, whose students would not merely take it at face value. They believed that younger students might not understand the subtle message of the book. "They just react to the racist words and comments," one student said. "They don't realize that the book is really against racism."

It was that kind of influence that Earl had hoped the club would have when he started it. As a senior, about to graduate, he knew it would not benefit him directly, but he hoped it would have some impact by the time his younger sister reached high school. "Nothing will get done to change things if we don't get involved," he says. "It bothers me when people say there are no racial problems in Plano. There are. But they're subtle, and we can't let subtle racism continue. We have to come together, gather the facts, and present a united front to issues. If we do it thoughtfully and with careful planning, it will work."

Jean Edwards, the media librarian at the school, is one of the adult sponsors of the Ethnic Club. Earl knew about her involvement in the "I Have a Dream" Program in Dallas and thought she would be receptive to his idea for the club. She was, and now she is as enthusiastic as the students. "We've needed this awareness for some time," she says. "The only way we're going to accept each other is to learn to understand each other."

The organization still has only fifteen to twenty members, but Venus West, the current president, has hope for the future. "As the years go by and the club has some age to it, it will grow," she says.

Venus joined the club because she believes in its purpose. But she also joined out of family tradition. "We've always been involved," she says. "We feel that we have to give back to the community. To all the people in it, not just people from our ethnic background."

Living up to that tradition, Venus has helped organize a joint tutoring venture with the Honor Society. It is aimed toward students with English as a second language, and the response has been good. Students come for help in their classes and also find support in other areas of adjusting to the school.

Venus thinks it is important that the club be about more than ethnic issues. "We don't want to limit our focus," she says. "That almost makes us exclusive. Last Christmas we had a party where everyone had to bring canned goods to give to the AIDS Research Center. That way the other kids know we're not just about one issue."

The Ethnic Club is not the only organization in Plano that is trying to make a difference. A similar organization at Plano East Senior High, the Junior Multi-Ethnic Committee, was formed in February 1990. It is modeled after the school district's Multi-Ethnic Committee. Both groups make recommendations on race-related incidents and seek to improve race relations.

On campus, the students believe that awareness is the key to racial harmony. "We feel it's important for us to know each other," Normita Joven says. "We all have so much in common and don't even realize it."

To get to know each other better, members of the Committee plan and host an awareness month for each ethnic group at the school. They have recognized the Asian and Hispanic communities and even had an Oktoberfest cosponsored by the German Club.

This group also tries not to be limited in its purpose. The

members believe that it is through education and awareness that the most progress will be made. "We've accomplished so much already," Normita says. "When we have awareness months, they become topics of discussion in class and things like that."

The benefit of "getting to know each other" seems to be a two-way street. Members of other groups get to meet new people and gain an appreciation of them and their culture. And the group being recognized that month feels a little special, gaining confidence and pride in who they are.

Another activity of both organizations is inviting speakers of different backgrounds to the school. Working with the administration, they utilize speakers in classes where most appropriate. "We want to show more ethnic diversity in the curriculum," Jean Edwards says. "History, for example, should not be just from one perspective."

Similar groups are springing up in other areas of the country as more and more people realize the importance of doing something positive to curb racism. "It's up to us to improve our understanding of each other," Venus West says. "Then we can pass better racial values on to our kids. That's the way we can change things."

Some students in Denton, Texas, also decided to do something to change the situation in their junior high school. There had always been a lot of tension between Hispanic and white students. In 1987, following a fight, five of the students decided to find a constructive way to deal with their differences. They formed a new organization, Hispanic Pride, to create mutual respect and friendship. The route they chose was to embrace ethnic differences.

With the aid of a school counselor, Debbie Grindle, the group first sought self-pride. "We wanted the Hispanic students to develop a higher sense of self-esteem and to feel like part of the campus," Ms. Grindle said. "We wanted to give them a vehicle for socialization and a sense of being members of a group."

Other school officials agreed that the tensions were increased by frustration and alienation. Helping the Hispanic students gain a deeper sense of pride in their heritage would ease the frustration and, eventually, the tensions.

It worked. The organization has grown over the years, and there are fewer problems between Hispanic and white students. "It has helped a lot," says student Robert Ayala. "Before we would be pushing each other around, talking bad about each other. Now we're friends."

Willingness to confront the issues is not limited to junior high or high school students. Many college campuses are forming ethnic organizations to help students become aware of and appreciate the diversity of people.

In November 1990, students at Southern Methodist University in Dallas participated in an Intercultural Awareness Week, with an exercise in segregation. Red and blue buttons were assigned to students at random, red signifying the privileged majority and blue the oppressed minority.

Students with blue buttons had to sit in the rear of classrooms. They were not allowed to drink from water fountains and were restricted to a few tables in the cafeteria.

"The purpose was to allow students to experience what it is to live in a controlled environment," says Clarence Glover, director of intercultural education. "What I've heard them say is, 'This sucks.' In reality, that sums up segregation."

Experiencing or seeing firsthand what it means to suffer discrimination has a lasting impact. It is no longer a problem "out there" to which we can't relate. When we see it, taste it, feel it, it becomes our problem too.

That is what a high school teacher in New York realized in May 1990. There had been a lot of friction between African-Americans and Korean merchants over unresolved incidents of harassment, and Fred McCray decided to do something. What he did was take his students to lunch—at a Korean market.

They passed through the crowd that was boycotting the store and went in to buy food. It was a simple gesture, and perhaps it did no more than allow the students to see the Korean owner face to face. But McCray was harshly criticized by black community leaders. Wilbert Tatum, publisher of the *Amsterdam News*, accused McCray of "using" the students to break up a legitimate boycott.

Linda Ellerbee, who related the incident in her syndicated column, disagreed. "I say he's (Tatum) missed the point. What matters is that Fred McCray and some African-American high school students DID something about racism. They voted with their feet."

Other people are confronting the issues on a larger scale.

In 1985 the Anti-Defamation League in Boston launched a major project called "A World of Difference." Its goal is to increase awareness of prejudice and work on reducing it. Designed for community-wide participation, the program is being utilized in cities all across America.

It has two main focal points, education and exposure. The educational side centers around study guides that are distributed free to public and private schools. Each community that participates uses material designed to address its specific racial problems and tensions.

Educators, media people, and community leaders work with "World of Difference" people to develop each city's program. This is an important part of the overall project, according to Barbara Pitts, the Educational Coordinator in Dallas.

She previously worked with the program in New York before moving to Dallas, and she recognizes that each area has its own unique problems. "It would be unrealistic to think we could approach this city's problems the way we did in New York," she says.

Ms. Pitts has worked with a local team to prepare materials for use in the Dallas Independent School District. She is also in charge of the training sessions for teachers. In a six-hour voluntary training seminar teachers become familiar with the material and learn skills needed to work more effectively with minority students.

Following the training, the teachers use the material in social studies, humanities, and some English classes. Whenever a prejudice-related issue comes up, it is discussed. "Often people aren't aware of an issue," Ms. Pitts said, "or at least not the specifics of it. This way people are acknowledging certain problems and looking at constructive ways to deal with them."

The other focus of *"A World of Difference"* is on awareness through media support. In Dallas the program is supported by WFAA-TV and the Dallas *Morning News*. Throughout 1990 the television station aired public service announcements in which people talked about their experience with racial issues. Longer programs addressed a specific concern, such as sensitivity in the media.

In most cities that participate in "A World of Difference" a year-long commitment is made for media coverage and promotion. Ms. Pitts indicated that some sponsors choose to continue and have been running the program for several years.

Does it really make a difference? Ms. Pitts believes it does. "It won't change that much today, or next week," she says. "But over the long term, it will. It took years and years to get where we are today; it's going to take a while to get past it."

To live peacefully together in a multicultural society, we need to see what we have in common as well as respect our different life-styles and traditions. Have you ever celebrated Hanukkah or Passover with Jewish friends, or Christmas or Easter with Christian friends? Have you ever eaten soul food or sung gospel hymns? Sometimes it helps to do something as simple as that.

In the spring of 1989 in Dallas, hundreds of people took part in a project called "Crossroads," sponsored by the Greater Dallas Council of Churches and PBS television station KERA. The program centered around pairing members of different churches who would visit each other's church and participate in services and discussion.

A wide variety of denominations participated, and it was a mingling of color and culture, as well as religion. Members of predominantly white congregations paired with black churches, and most participants found it a rewarding, awakening experience.

"It may sound strange," said one Catholic participant, "but I never thought of Baptists as people. They were just this other group. Going to their service and talking one on one, I realized we're more alike than I thought. The fact that they were black added another dimension. I had never talked to a black person about religion. I guess I had never really *talked* to a black person at all."

Many of the white people who had not had much contact with people from other cultures admitted that it was a bit intimidating at first to be a stranger among strangers. But they were aware of the need for change and believed in the project, so they accepted the challenge.

It is through projects like "Crossroads" and "A World of Difference," coupled with individual efforts, that progress will be made. Government agencies and legislation cannot solve the problem alone. They are too far removed from the basics. The problem of racism is a *people* problem and can only be solved by people.

What can you do if there are no organized programs or projects you can get involved in?

First of all, you could start a program at your school. Barbara Pitts suggests working through your student council president, who is already in a recognized position of leadership. The student council president has the means to communicate with the administration and be heard.

If you don't have time to make that kind of commitment, you can do other things. Perhaps you could get a group of friends together on a Saturday afternoon and paint over racist graffiti around the school.

You could write letters to television producers who promote stereotypes in programming. That, too, is something you could get a group together to do in an afternoon.

At a party or other gathering you could speak out against bigoted remarks or jokes.

You could encourage your church to be more involved in combatting bigotry. Ask your pastor to preach about the injustice of prejudice. Maybe your youth group could pair with a youth group from another denomination as the people did in the "Crossroads" project. Or maybe the group would like to adopt an immigrant family from the Middle East or South America.

Whatever you decide to do, it is important to do something. The battle is not lost unless we give up.

Progress has been made through the efforts of people who believed they could make a difference. Some of them were well known; others were everyday folks who decided maybe not to change the world, but simply to change themselves.

No matter how they are doing it, people are learning that different can be okay.

CHAPTER 10

Guess Who's Coming to Dinner?

Unfortunately, not a great deal has changed since the 1968 film "Guess Who's Coming to Dinner?" dramatized the reactions to an interracial marriage. True, the most obvious racial mix, black and white, does not create quite the sensation it did a generation ago, but it is still not always accepted.

Acceptance is determined by attitudes, and as long as we have bigotry there will not be total acceptance.

The depth of the attitude controls the strength of the reaction. Clint says his parents wouldn't consider it a family crisis if he had a black girlfriend. "I think they'd have some concerns, but I don't think they would say anything derogatory or tell me I couldn't see her".

Debbie*, on the other hand, faces a much more serious problem. Her father is extremely bigoted, and as long as she can remember it has been a real issue between them.

* Name has been changed.

Now she is planning to marry a black man, and, as she puts it, "My dad is going to have a fit."

From the time Debbie was a little girl she objected to her father's racial slurs and comments. When he referred to a black man as a "nigger," she told him that wasn't nice, that he shouldn't do that. He just laughed and said she was silly.

Their opposing views were not much of a problem when she was a cute five-year-old sitting on Dad's knee watching TV. But as she grew older they created some real difficulties. Her father no longer found her objections amusing, and she grew frustrated that he was never willing to see her point.

"I don't know how or why I had different attitudes," Debbie says. "Both my parents are prejudiced, and most of their families were. But I just knew prejudice was wrong."

The whole issue might not have been more than a difference of opinions between Debbie and her parents if it were not for her boyfriend, Tom*. Their mutual interest in basketball first brought them together in college, and for a long time they were just friends. That was common with Debbie even in high school. Most of her friends were guys, some of them black, and basketball was the common interest.

Then Debbie realized that her friendship with Tom had evolved into something more. They began to discuss the possibility of getting married.

If Tom were not black, she would have no hesitation in telling her parents about her plans. But knowing her father's attitudes, she keeps putting if off. "I know he's going to blow a gasket," she says with a laugh. "The question is, when. Do I tell him now and get it over with, or wait until our plans are firmer?"

Debbie pauses for a moment to think of the ideal way the

situation could be handled. "I wish Tom lived closer. [He lives several hundred miles away.] Then Mom and Dad could meet him and get to know him for who he is. Maybe when they were more comfortable with him as a person, not just a black person, they wouldn't be angry and upset."

The reality, as Debbie sees it, is that her father will turn away from her completely. She accepts that, and intellectually she is ready to deal with it. As she says, "I've got to be my own person. This is my life and my decision."

But the little girl who sat on her Daddy's knee is going to have a hard time reconciling all of it in the future. "I know it's not going to be easy," she says, tears threatening to spill out of her eyes. "But he's wrong. He's always been wrong. And it would be wrong for me to deny my life because of his attitudes."

From Tom's point of view, the problems are less severe. His family has accepted Debbie, and no one has voiced any objection to their plans. They have expressed some concern over the obvious problem of Debbie's family. Is Tom aware of how stressful that will be? Are they going to be able to face the issues and work through them?

Debbie says they spend a lot of time talking about those problems. They don't want to get married until they know, or at least think, they are ready to handle it all.

The potential for problems seems to be greater in a black/white mix than in any other mix. Part of the reason is that it's so obvious. But even when it's not, it still can draw the strongest reactions.

Laura, a very light-skinned African-American, has been married to a very dark Italian for over twenty years. Two of their children are dark, one is fair. Laura recalls that when the children were younger people would stare at the whole family. "They would look at each one of the kids, then back at me. Then they would look at Chris [her husband] and sort of nod as if to say, "Ah, that's why they're so dark.""

"I would almost want to laugh," she continues. "At first it would be sort of comical watching them try to figure it out. Then I'd get annoyed. I resented the fact that they thought they had a right to know."

That assumption on the part of strangers has even led to questions. Some people ask if the children are adopted, especially the son who is so fair. "I don't mind if a friend asks questions," Laura says. "Curiosity is normal. But when it comes to a stranger invading someone's privacy it's no longer normal curiosity. It would be like my going up to someone at the mall and saying, 'Why are you so fat?' It's none of my business."

The reasons for such strong reactions to the mix of black and white are many. Most of them you probably have figured out for yourself based on the history of prejudice we covered earlier. The accumulation of stereotypes and attitudes plays a big part. But other myths specifically associated with the idea of socializing and marriage come into play.

During the period of colonization of America, the black slaves were considered more carnal than "genteel" people. What was normal and natural for the African in his own country in dress and behavior was seen as "subhuman" in the new environment. The slave owners began to think of the slaves as animals, and a myth emerged that they were "creatures of unbridled passion." It seemed to be the only explanation for the slaves' lack of concern for modesty and decorum.

Like all myths, people tended to use this one as it suited them best for the moment. Applying it to slave women somehow made it okay for the white owners to take them into their beds. Servicing the master was part of what the women were expected to do, and since they had all that passion it must be something they wanted to do.

However, that same passion and lustiness in the black man was not considered normal and natural. It was seen as sexual aggression.

In *The White Man's Burden*, Winthrop D. Jordan writes that that idea stemmed primarily from the white man's guilt over his own sexual aggression. Taking the slave women to bed was widely practiced at the time, but not widely accepted. People knew it was done, but it was not talked about or openly acknowledged.

For that reason, Jordan believes, the fear of black men lusting after white women was based on guilt. There was no other evidence to support the fear, and few, if any, incidents of such actions. Even during periods of slave uprisings, when plenty of opportunities arose, white women were not abused by the slaves.

The double standard people applied to this issue was as damaging as any double standard can be. Added to the puritanical attitudes most people had, it created more myths that still influence our thinking.

Debbie is aware that a lot of "background garbage" influences the way people react to her and Tom. She has heard all the jokes and comments, but she wishes it didn't have to be that way. "Why does it have to be a *white* woman and a *black* man?" she asks. "Why can't it just be me and Tom, two people who love each other and want to make a life together. None of that other stuff should even be a part of it."

Ideally, she's right. Our lives and relationships would be far less complicated if we didn't have to deal with anything beyond this moment in time. But life just doesn't work that way.

Every relationship is affected by outside forces, and it takes more than just deciding to get married to make it work. When you are also blending ethnic backgrounds, the challenge is even greater. Not because we shouldn't blend, but because the blending is so hard sometimes. For all the things we have in common as human beings, differences in culture can cause conflict.

Many groups of people have traditions and customs that are unique to their heritage. Some of them are obvious, and some are more subtle. We have to be aware of those customs and understand how they will affect us on a day-to-day basis. For example, in Oriental philosophy women are held in great esteem, but they are not expected to be aggressive or forward.

Your Chinese boyfriend, who was raised in the United States, may accept Western standards and Western women, but his family is still "old country." What you see in yourself as normal behavior they could completely misunderstand. They could even be insulted by something you say that you had no idea could be interpreted that way.

Perhaps you think that doesn't have to be a problem. You're marrying Chim, not his family. But that is not entirely true. When people marry, they don't live in a vacuum. It is not just the two of you, and a lot of problems in marriages come from difficulties with other family members.

To make the blending easier, it would be good to study Oriental culture and philosophy. That way you could understand why his family has certain expectations that are alien to you. You could also learn to be more tolerant of the differences between you and find a way not to let them be an issue all the time.

That is what Jimmy did with his family and his wife. "When we had family gatherings we just avoided the fact that Claudie is Jewish," he says. "That way we didn't have to argue about the things we didn't agree on."

Making an effort really to know about the other person's culture can also show a deeper level of commitment. It is almost like saying, "This is how much I care about you. I'm willing to spend my time finding out everything I can."

Mike, a college student in Austin who is dating a Hispanic girl, says that his interest in her background has enhanced their relationship. "We talk about all the things that are different from what I'm used to," he says. "And I've really gained an appreciation of Spanish culture. I think that appreciation is important to her, because it shows respect. I don't have a frivolous attitude toward things that matter to her."

Mutual respect is a key element in successful relationships. It can also play a crucial role in effectively blending two cultures. Sometimes when we don't understand something about the other person we make a joke about it. That only belittles the other person. Then he may start pulling away, and pretty soon a great chasm divides us.

When we have mutual respect and appreciation, it helps us to feel good about ourselves. It also helps us to feel good about the other person. It makes us more willing to work toward a mutually satisfying resolution to the problems we face.

Those are some of the ways you can make it better for you, but what about your parents? If you are thinking about marrying someone of a different ethnic background, there are bound to be problems. Your parents may not understand. They could even try to talk you out of it, and acceptance could come slowly.

If your parents are as strongly prejudiced as Debbie's, you may have to decide whether you are willing to risk a complete break in the relationship with them. Sometimes it comes to that, and like Debbie, you have to be sure of yourself and your ability to handle it.

In handling it, it helps not to feel guilty. You have to keep reminding yourself that it is not your problem. It is their problem, especially if you have been over the same issues time and again and they are not willing to bend.

It is also possible that in time things will change. Some people just take longer than others to adjust. If you are patient, a time will come when things are not so terrible.

If your parents are more like Clint's there is a better chance your plans won't cause total alienation. That does not mean there won't be problems, but they should be easier to deal with.

You will have to take your cue from how well your family handles other problems. If you communicate well and have healthy methods of operating, you should be able to work through this.

Whenever a conflict does arises, you can utilize the methods covered in Chapter 6 for resolving it.

Another suggestion is not to confront the conflict immediately. Our reactions tend to be controlled by anger and hurt, and we instinctively want to hurt back.

If your parents tell you they don't want you to date your friend of another ethnic background, it will make you mad. When you are mad you will not be able to be rational about the situation. You'll be more apt to snap something like, "That's not fair. I'll do what I want."

Your parents' response will probably be something like, "Now just one minute. As long as you live in this house, you'll do as I say."

Now you have lost sight of the issue entirely, and no one is going to be reasonable.

By waiting until your initial anger and resentment ease off, you may be able to talk to your parents constructively. Perhaps you can explain how much this person means in your life right now, and ask them to give it a chance. Remind them that you are old enough to make such a decision for yourself.

Talking that way may be "pie in the sky" under most circumstances, but it might be worth a try. It would at least be better than shouting at each other.

In cross-culture dating it is also wise not to look for trouble where none exists. At times we are so sensitive about things that we create an atmosphere of conflict by our sensitivity. When we are too defensive, we often assign nonexistent motives to the other person. That can lead to a build-up of resentment that prevents us from recognizing when the other person is making an effort to improve the situation.

For instance, if you have your friend over for dinner and Dad is a little reserved, you may think it's because he doesn't want your friend there. That may not be the reason at all. Perhaps your father is just feeling awkward because it is such a new experience for him. If he has never had a one-on-one contact with someone of a different background, he may not know what to say or how to act. By deciding for yourself what your father is thinking, you only convince yourself that nothing will change.

Every situation in life seems to call for a great balancing act, and this one is no exception. You have to find a way to keep from reacting to emotions without backing down from a legitimate confrontation. You have to try to separate issues from feelings and look at everything in the most reasonable light.

It will not be easy. Sometimes it will be downright tough, and you may think nothing will ever change. But if you persevere, you may get lucky. Like Jimmy, you may find in time that your parents come to accept someone who is different in your life and theirs.

CHAPTER 11

Just Friends

Socializing covers a lot more than intimate relationships and marriage. We are pulled together in all kinds of situations, and how we interact has a lot to do with what we bring with us. Are we reserved and suspicious, or open and friendly?

Paul, a high school sophomore, first met his African-American friend in sixth grade. He had known other black kids all through grade school and junior high but never really got to be friends. Then Fred started hanging around with Paul and another friend, Joey. "Fred was just an all-right guy," Paul says. "He was fun to be around, and I never thought about color. It just didn't matter.

"There are other black kids I don't like," Paul continues. "But it doesn't have anything to do with their being black. There was one guy in choir with me who exaggerated all the time to show off. He was always acting like a big shot, and I didn't like him. But a lot of white guys act the same way, and I don't like them either."

What Paul likes about Fred is that he's a good friend. He can be trusted. They have a good time together. And Fred does not have an attitude about other white guys. He is willing to give everyone a chance not to be racist without looking for problems where there aren't any.

A lot went into the forming of that friendship that Paul was never even aware of. Certain dynamics occur when people meet that either make them attractive as friends or not. Those dynamics happen on an unconscious level as we make our choices in friendships.

It might be helpful to understand from a scientific viewpoint what some of those dynamics are. In either short- or long-term relationships, people go through various stages of acceptance.

The first stage is *initial contact*. That deals with first reactions that prompt you either to pursue a friendship or not. Perhaps something about the person makes you want to know him or her better, or perhaps it is just a feeling.

In all friendships, whether romantic or not, some attraction drew you together. Something made you say, "This person seems kind of nice. Maybe we could be friends." For Paul it was the fact that he could feel so comfortable around Fred.

On the other hand, certain things make us shy away from other people. It may be something intangible; you can't say for sure what it is. But something makes you pull away and decide that you would not be interested in a friendship with that person.

At other times you are quite sure why you don't want to pursue a friendship. Like Paul, you can name several reasons without even thinking hard.

The next stage is *competition*. In every situation where we relate to other people, there are times when we compete. We do it between brothers and sisters, vying for our parents' attention. We do it among our groups when we feel we have to compete with one for the acceptance of another.

If we understand that this is a natural part of relationships, it becomes easier to deal with. It does not have to destroy our family or our friendships.

Accommodation is the next stage of relationship, and it helps us deal with the competition. When people are accommodating to each other they are willing to adapt to someone else's needs. Not just focused on their own desires, they are better able to settle differences equitably.

Being able to be accommodating can take the sharp edge off our competition, especially in family situations. Most of the time when we feel we have to fight for our parents' attention, it is because we feel particularly insecure and vulnerable. That insecurity may make us feel resentful. Because of our resentment, we are centered on ourselves, and we may often see favoritism where there isn't any.

Instead of getting angry at our parents for making us feel miserable, perhaps we can reevaluate the situation. Usually we are responsible for the way we feel, not someone else. Although it sometimes feels as if our parents are being partial to our brother, they probably are not.

We can also help ourselves by realizing that there are times when one child in the family needs more attention than the others. It is not that our parents love our brother more; it's just that he is getting ready to go off to college and he's scared. He *needs* our parents more. Understanding that makes it easier to let him have the extra attention without feeling left out. It should also reassure us that our parents will be there for us when we need them most.

The final stage of relationship is *assimilation*. In the broadest sense, the word means people living harmoniously with a full sense of belonging. When applied to immigrants, it means becoming fully absorbed in the homeland. When applied to socializing, it means being totally accepted within the group.

We can help or hinder the process of assimilation depending on how we interact with people who happen to be different. If our association with other ethnic groups is purely casual, it may never rise above a superficial level. At that level, it may do nothing to dispel prejudicial attitudes. In fact, some experts believe it can even reinforce prejudice.

In *The Nature of Prejudice*, Gordon Allport suggests that if we never get beyond our initial reaction to someone from another ethnic group, we have no way of countering our prejudgments. To illustrate the point he uses an example of a Jew and an Irishman who have a casual business encounter.

Because of long-standing attitudes, the Irishman thinks, "Ah, a Jew. Perhaps he'll skin me. I'll be careful."

Likewise the Jew thinks, "Probably a Mick. They hate the Jews. I'll have to watch him."

The outcome is that both men approach each other with evasiveness and distrust. They have no realistic basis for those feelings; it's all prejudgment. By the cool reserve thay have toward each other, they confirm their suspicions and leave matters worse than before.

The only solution, then, is to get past the suspicion, the prejudgment, and meet each other as equals.

Paul does not understand why we don't do that now. Nor does he understand why discrimination exists. What makes people act the way they do toward each other? "All people should be treated with a courtesy that goes deeper than just, 'Have a nice day'," he says. "We should relate to each other more than just what's on the surface."

Danielle, a high school junior, agrees. Speaking of one of her best friends, Danielle says that at first she didn't notice

Angel was black. "Of course, I *saw* that she was black, but it really didn't hit me. I saw the inside of her. I saw a friend."

Barry, another high school junior, notes that the immediate ability to see beyond color is what is so neat about young children. "Little kids don't pay any attention to those characteristics," he says. "It doesn't matter to them until they're taught differently."

Socializing has been difficult for Minh, a high school junior who was born in Vietnam. He has been in the United States since he was about ten, and he and his parents have experienced a lot of discrimination. When Minh was in seventh grade he had an especially hard time with another boy who kept calling him an "Ethiopian Chink."

"My parents set me up with the school counselor," Minh says. "But they talked to me, too. They asked why I thought that guy was good enough to call me that. They firmed up the attitude that I shouldn't think those comments made me any less than other people."

Some people still make fun of Minh, but he has learned to handle it better. He is not so apprehensive about what people might say or how they might treat him at a party. "Basically, I just shrug the comments off, or I turn them around. Someone may say, 'Hey, Chink,' and I say, 'Yeah, and proud of it. What are you proud of?'"

Minh has found some healthy ways to deal with his frustration over incidents of discrimination. He tries to look at the good things that happen, to focus on the people who are nice. But when things do build up, he doesn't strike out; he takes it out on his punching bag.

Most of the young people who talked about their experiences agreed that you have to watch what you do with your anger. When people say something ugly to you, your instinct is to retaliate either verbally or physically, but that doesn't help the situation.

Barry recalls an incident in seventh grade that taught him that important lesson.

"I was wrestling with this one guy. Actually, we were fighting because we just didn't like each other. And I had him in a head lock.

"This other guy comes by and says, 'A fight, a fight, a nigger and a white,' and I went, 'What?'

"I was already pretty pumped up, and I shouldn't have let myself get out of control. But I said, 'Excuse me!' Then I popped him."

Barry admits that he is not very proud of what he did. In fact, he says, he realized almost immediately that it was pretty stupid.

Minh finds it easier to socialize in small groups with kids he knows than in a big party. That is probably true for all of us, whether we are crossing cultural bounds or not.

If you have ever been in a school play you know how it is in the beginning. You are all a bit reserved, approaching new contacts with caution. Things are awkward for everyone.

But by the time the cast party rolls around it's as if you have all been best friends forever. You have spent so much time together and worked so hard for a common goal that you have gained a sense of unity. Everyone is comfortable in the group, and any surface differences no longer matter.

Another factor that makes socializing easier is sensitivity about racial remarks or jokes that promote stereotypes. Within your own ethnic group certain words are used that are not acceptable outside the group. On the surface that may seem like a double standard. As Tony commented in an earlier chapter, "Why is it okay for a black guy to call another black guy a 'nigger', but a white guy can't?"

Barry thinks it has to do with the connotation, or the intent behind use of the word. "Within your own group you know what the person means. Outside the group you're not so sure."

Jessica suggests that it has a lot to do with the sensitiveness of the person hearing the word. Instead of thinking of it as just a word, the person reads into it an intent that wasn't there.

Racial jokes can take different directions. Sometimes friends share jokes and no offense is taken. Other times someone seems to be slamming a minority. Intent to insult is different from just playing around.

Clint thinks the key to making jokes is how comfortable the people are with each other. He says that his close friends tell cripple jokes all the time. "But it doesn't bother me. I know they don't mean anything bad. They respect me and who I am. The jokes are all in fun."

Joking can sometimes diffuse awkwardness between people. Michael, who is one of Clint's close friends, says that at first he felt uneasy about referring to Clint's physical challenge. "Then Clint made a joke about his crutches one day and that broke the ice."

Speaking of jokes that point out stereotypes, Michael thinks they can be okay as long as everyone in the group knows the stereotype is not true. "Then you're laughing at the stereotype," he says, "not the people."

Robert thinks that joking is acceptable only as long as you know why you are doing it. "If you're doing it to keep the stereotype alive, that's not right," he says. "But if you're doing it to point out how silly and ridiculous it is, that's okay."

It is obvious in this touchy area of jokes and comments that everyone has to use a great deal of common sense. We all know when we are about to step over the bounds of courtesy and respect. If something inside warns us not to tell a certain joke, perhaps we shouldn't. If we make a remark and instantly feel embarrassed, maybe we should think before we make such a remark again.

Another subject that should be considered as part of socializing is cross-culture dating. That need not mean serious relationships, but merely people who may be interested in casual dating outside their race.

Oprah Winfrey discussed this subject on a panel show on February 5, 1991. The young people in the audience were less tolerant of interracial dating than the older people.

It was a very controversial show, with strong emotional reactions from people who had not dated outside their race. It was also filled with apparent double standards. The white man who dated black women was considered "cool." The black man who dated whites was accused of being a "wimp."

One panel member made the point that she was not trying to make a social statement by her dating choices. "We shouldn't be worried about who is dating whom," she said. "Color should not be an issue. It is a personal preference like short versus tall."

Some audience members refused to see it so simply. They accused the panel members of denying their own culture by dating outside it.

The members of the audience who had dated outside their race seemed to understand the attitudes of the panel better than others. Perhaps that was because they appeared more secure in themselves and were able to speak fairly reasonably. They were not so defensive of their own race and did not attack the panel verbally. Others accused them of perpetuating the stereotypes and contributing to racism.

To counter that, one man said that before he had dated outside his race he had been very prejudiced against blacks. Now that he has dated a few black women, he said, he has been able to get beyond his prejudice in general.

Early in the program Oprah posed the question, "Does interracial dating promote racism and stereotypes?" It was interesting to note that the dating itself had less influence than people's reactions to it. Audience members, and even Oprah herself, brought up the stereotypes.

When panelists denied that their interest in someone of another race had to do with stereotypes, audience reaction was, "Oh, sure." It was obvious that they had already made up their minds.

That is a perfect example of how closed-mindedness keeps the problems of racism alive. If we lived in a perfect world it wouldn't happen, but we all have to learn to adapt to the imperfections.

If you date or have friends from other ethnic backgrounds, you may run into that closed-mindedness. Like Minh, you have to know when it is best to shrug it off and when you can challenge it. It will be considerably less frustrating if you are not spinning your wheels against a hopeless situation.

CHAPTER ◇ 12

Taking a Risk

C hanging is something that many people find extremely hard to do. It means making some sort of effort, and usually it is easier just to stay the way we are. The greater the challenge to change, the more reluctant most of us are.

In the area of prejudice the same rule applies. Extremely bigoted people put up the hardest fight against the idea of change and are probably also more unreasonable in their arguments against it.

Debbie says she gave up trying to change her parents' attitudes a long time ago. "We used to get into these screaming matches. Especially Dad. He would say I had no right to tell him what to do, and I felt that the issue was too important to ignore. But it didn't do any good. Eventually, I realized it was easier on both of us if I just shut up.

"Sometimes I felt bad about giving up, but I knew it wasn't making any difference. All it was doing was keeping the tension between us all the time. And it was influencing everything. Basically, we just needed a break."

One thing to keep in mind in talking about change is that it is impossible to change another person, at least in the sense that most of us think of it. We cannot *make* another person do something he or she does not want to. We can ask for change, encourage change, influence change, but we cannot change anyone but ourselves.

That is a reality that bothers many people. If we could just *fix* the other person, the problem would go away. Perhaps you have run across it in your own experience. You get mad at your best friend when she tells something you told her in confidence. "Why can't you learn to keep your mouth shut?" you scream at her.

Every time the problem comes up between you, you think there has to be a way you can make her respect your confidences. If you talk to her one more time, surely she will realize how important it is. She'll learn. She'll change.

What is happening is that you are trying to take responsibility for her problem, and you cannot do it. The problem is hers. It does you no good to get mad at her every time she runs off at the mouth. Your problem is thinking that she'll stop if you yell at her enough.

Perhaps the best way to solve that problem is to accept the way she is and stop telling her your secrets. That eliminates *your* problem, and you no longer have to worry about *hers*.

That example illustrates an approach to coping with problems that has gained wide respect among mental health professionals. It is based on the certainty that people cannot change each other. All they can do is change a situation or their reaction to it.

Does that mean that you just leave your parents alone, that you do nothing to try to alter their way of thinking? Not necessarily. Remember, you can *influence* people to change. You can increase their awareness until they are able to change themselves.

But don't expect an instant cure. Prejudice is so much a

part of a person's personality and life experience that we cannot expect the change to come easily.

Jimmy Hudson made that mistake when he was very young. With the idealism of youth, he believed that his grandparents and parents would see the light if he tried hard enough. After all, they were basically good people. With the right kind of information, good people can eventually come to see the injustice of their attitudes.

According to Gordon Allport, that depends on how deeply embedded those attitudes are. People whose characteristics make them more tolerant are more willing to accept the idea of change. Given the right information, they can decide for themselves that they were wrong.

On the other hand, people who fit the personality profile of extreme prejudice seldom come to any personal willingness to change. By their very nature they are rigid and unyielding, firmly believing they are right. Trying to talk to them about the issue will probably be as disappointing as when Kelly tried to talk to her parents.

Margaret Singh, who has twelve years of experience as a school psychologist, agrees. "People who are extremely prejudiced are closed individuals. They aren't going to have the openness that would allow for a healthy discussion."

Sometimes you can confront other family members about their bigotry. Jessica, a junior in high school, had an experience with her grandfather that worked out well.

When she was thirteen Jessica wrote a paper about American Indians for a school assignment. She did a good report and was excited about the grade she received. She wanted her grandfather to read the paper, but he just put it aside.

"I had absolutely no idea he was prejudiced," Jessica says. "So at first I didn't know that was why he didn't want to read my paper. I was just hurt because I was so proud of getting a hundred and he wouldn't even look at it. Anyway, I finally told him that if he didn't read it I'd never speak to him again."

Jessica also told him she realized that he had formed his ideas in a different time, that he was influenced by ideas that were acceptable then. She said that she understood, but that things were different now and he didn't have to keep thinking that way. She emphasized how important it was to her personally that he read her report and then repeated her threat.

It worked. Jessica's grandfather did read the report, and he talked to her about some of the points she had made. Since then he has done a lot of research on his own and no longer views the American Indian the way he did before.

Jessica is very proud that she had that kind of influence with her grandfather, but she also realizes that she could not do the same thing with her parents.

Margaret Singh agrees. "For one thing," she says, "it's hard at thirteen to threaten never to speak to your parents again. You've got to live with them for a few more years, and that's real hard to do without talking."

But Ms. Singh also explains that having the relationship once removed makes it easier. Grandparents are often more receptive to a challenge than a parent would be. Parents are locked into that "authority" struggle that is so much a part of normal parent/child relationships. "If Jessica had tried that with her parents, they'd have probably sent her to her room."

At this point, you should be able to judge for yourself whether or not you can confront this issue with your parents. And if they are extremely bigoted, the advice is against confronting them.

Robert, a twenty-two-year-old college student, agrees. "It's hard to push on something you know will be a conflict," he says. "It seems we're already in conflict over so much. Why add to the frustration?"

With parents who are not extremely bigoted, there might be some benefit in trying to discuss your differences. You must decide for yourself based on past experience in talking to them about difficult things.

If you do decide to bring it into the open, you might want to approach it indirectly. Gordon Allport says it is wiser to attack discrimination than to attack prejudice. Perhaps you could talk to your parents about some recent incident of discrimination. Make it a discussion about the issue, not a personal confrontation over values.

Clint found that this approach worked with his parents. He didn't bring up their attitudes or make judgments; he just started dropping hints. "I didn't say anything like, 'Gee, I wish you weren't so prejudiced.' I just wouldn't let a racist remark get by. If they made some comment, I'd say, 'Hey, they're just people.'"

It hasn't made a big difference, Clint admits, but it's a beginning. His parents don't make as many racist remarks as they once did. Now he thinks the time may be right actually to talk to them about their attitudes. That is mainly because he is older now. He has been away at college for a couple of years, and their whole way of relating has changed.

Robert also finds it easier to talk to his parents about issues now than when he was living at home. "It's like we have a more equal relationship. They treat me more like an adult, and they respect my opinion even when we disagree."

Talking may be the best approach in challenging parents who are only slightly bigoted. Unfortunately, however, many contemporary families cannot seem to talk to each other, for a variety of reasons. One psychologist believes that the percentage of teens who cannot talk to their parents may be as high as ninety percent.

Chris considers himself lucky that he can talk to his parents. Most of his good friends can, too, but he does know some kids who cannot. He thinks part of the reason is that the parents are not home a lot.

Chris's mother agrees. She says it takes a great deal of time together to be able to really talk, especially about difficult issues. "When you know your kids, you can tell if something is bothering them, but they won't often come right out with it. I usually have to start talking around a lot of issues before I hit on the one that's causing a problem."

Even though Chris knows he can talk to his parents about almost anything, he says it is not always easy about a tough subject. "I can't just go up and say, 'Hey, Mom' and then tell her whatever . . ." he shrugs. "It's hard."

One thing Chris never thought of was developing a strategy for talking about those difficult things. Thinking through a plan for bringing up a sensitive issue can make it easier.

So let's pretend that you are like Chris and think you can talk to your parents most of the time. Let's also pretend that your parents have a few racist attitudes that bother you, and you would like to introduce that issue.

You need to pick a good time, of course. Bringing it up when they are busy or distracted would not get good results. Try to choose a time when they are relaxed, perhaps right after dinner when everyone is still gathered around the table.

Another approach is to ask for a family meeting. If you

already get together to discuss issues that affect the family, you have an advantage. You can use that time to introduce your concern about bigotry. In an already established forum, your parents may be more willing to listen and take you seriously.

Whichever method you choose, it is important to remember some of the principles we covered in Chapter 6 about problem-solving:

- Stick to the issue.
- Respect each other.
- Be willing to compromise.
- Work for a win/win solution.
- Remember what is at stake.

Above all, do not put your parents on the defensive. Do not accuse, blame, or criticize them as you introduce the subject. Choose your words carefully and avoid using phrases like, "You're wrong . . . You shouldn't . . ." that are sure to get a strong emotional response from your parents.

A good way to get started might be to introduce the general subject of racism and discrimination. You could say something like, "You know, it really bothers me to see discrimination."

"Oh, yeah? Like what?"

"Well, like the way everybody treats this new kid at school. No one hangs around with him because he's Vietnamese, and they all make fun of him."

"Maybe they leave him alone because he wants it that way."

"But how do they know that? They haven't even given him a chance. They're just acting on what they think they know about him. And that's not fair."

"Well, it's certainly not the end of the world. It's just one boy in one isolated incident."

"But it's not really. It happens to lots of people. And everyone lets it happen."

"So now you're going to be a crusader?"

"No. It just bothers me, that's all. Racism isn't going to stop until each person recognizes his part in it."

On the surface it may seem that the conversation did not accomplish much. The parent did not come to an awesome realization of how wrong he or she was. In fact, nothing was even said about his or her racism. So what good did it do?

Well, it got the subject out in the open for perhaps the first time. It also did so without antagonizing the parent. There was no personal attack or counterattack, no blaming, judging, or criticizing. Throughout the dialogue the focus stayed on the issue, so maybe it was a good first step. There may be other opportunities in the future to discuss the issues further.

Perhaps the next time you talk about it you can express how you feel about your parents' bigotry. Maybe you can even ask if they could be more aware of how it affects you.

Issues between parents and teens are seldom solved in one session. That is true no matter which side you are on. Chris's mother says she has found that the issues have become more complex as her children have gotten older. "I can't solve a problem with a one-time fix as I could when they were younger. Now the problems seem to be more ongoing. The same issues keep coming up over and over again."

That may not surprise you if you already are aware of that happening in your own life. How often have you had what seems like the same discussion with your parents over curfews, or grades, or the state of your room?

The same ongoing process of looking at the issue more than once will probably be the most effective way of talking to your parents about their racial attitudes. There is no one-time fix for that problem either.

OTHER THOUGHTS ABOUT CHANGE

Even though "A World of Difference" is trying to be an effective force against racism, its goal is not to force change. It points no fingers, places no blame, and does not focus on past injustice. It simply tries to draw people together to consider the problems of today and what can be done to solve them. And in educating the young people, it does not encourage them to try to change their parents.

"We never tell kids that their parents are wrong," says Barbara Pitts. "We don't want to take away respect for parents. We try to explain that the parents' attitudes are a result of the environment they grew up in. Parents can change only if their life experience changes."

In the whole area of change, Ms. Pitts suggests to young people, "Take a look at your own attitudes, at the things you learned from your parents. If there are some things you don't like or agree with, you can change yourself. You can move away from judging people from what you've heard."

Part of the emphasis in the educational programs is on making choices based on new information and a greater understanding of other ethnic groups. Through her years of experience with the program, Ms. Pitts is encouraged by the choices some kids are now making. She also emphasizes that in each generation things do change.

Phyllis Watson, a producer for WFAA-TV, firmly believes that attitudes can be changed with the right approach. She was responsible for "A World of Difference" programming that included hour-long specials as well as short spots in which individuals spoke briefly about their own experiences.

During the year-long series the station received hundreds of letters. Many expressed gratitude for programming that made them aware of their prejudice and gave them a desire to change. "Not everyone's going to be like that. Some people are never going to change," Ms. Watson says. "But many of them will, especially if they are influenced by children."

Gordon Allport believes change will eventually come about through education, awareness, and personal experience. But he cautions against overemphasis on just one of those factors. Education will have less impact on an individual if nothing in his personal experience supports the new information.

If, for example, a mildly prejudiced person watches an informative program on race relations, he can easily dismiss the information when the program is over. If, however, that same person gets involved in a community project, the information becomes part of his reality. He may learn that his black or Asian neighbors are not really a threat after all. The television show *told* him they were not, but the community project *proved* it to him.

Despite the many difficulties our society has faced on the issue of prejudice, Allport believes in our ability to rise above it. In the closing paragraph of his book he writes, "America, on the whole, has been a staunch defender of the right to be the same or different, although it has fallen short in many of its practices."

His final question is, "Can citizens learn to seek their own welfare and growth, not at the expense of their fellow men, but in concert with them?"

That clearly indicates that the solution of the problems does not rest with agencies, government, or committees.

Each person has to take responsibility for what he or she can do to advance the cause of justice, or hold it back.

"The new generation can act differently and pass on better racial values to their kids," Venus West says. "In time, it would make a difference if everyone tried."

CHAPTER 13

It's Your Life

Differences need not destroy our families. We live with differences of varying degrees in all our relationships. Without them our lives would be pretty bland.

Because each person is unique, he or she brings a particular set of ideas to situations. That can cause conflicts or, as one woman put it, "interesting opportunities."

Each conflict can be an opportunity for us to learn a little more about ourselves and a little more about the other person. It is an opportunity either to step forward in the relationship or take a step back. The direction we take is in large part up to each of us.

We can be willing to work constructively through the problem, using the techniques covered in Chapter 6. Or we can close ourselves off in anger and hurt, refusing to work through it.

But it takes two to have a conflict and two to resolve it. What if the other person is not willing to make an effort?

By now you have a pretty good idea whether things are ever going to change between you and your parents over the issue of bigotry. Maybe you have tried to talk to them, and it didn't work. Or perhaps you realized that trying to talk to them would be a waste of time and effort. What are you supposed to do now?

Well, now you have to find a way to live with the situation without its being a major source of conflict between you. Lieberman and Hardie call it *making room for the difference.* They say that two factors are involved in every issue debate: *process,* and *content.* When people cannot resolve their difference in terms of content, they can come to a resolution in process.

In the simplest terms that means we can have disagreements without letting them tear us apart.

To illustrate the point, Lieberman and Hardie use the example of a dispute between a father and son over what the son wants to wear to a father/son dinner at school. One way the scene could play out is as follows:

Dad walks into the living room a few minutes before they are supposed to leave. His son is sitting there in blue jeans and a T-shirt.

"It's almost time to leave. Aren't you going to get ready?"

"I am ready."

"You're going like that?"

"Sure, what's wrong with it?"

"What's wrong with it! You're supposed to wear decent clothes to a dinner like this. I want you to change right now."

In that exchange, neither of them said what was really important to him about the issue. The son did not express his uncertainty about what the rest of the guys would be wearing. What if he were the only one to show up in a suit and tie. They'd think he was a nerd. Doesn't his dad understand?

His dad never said anything about how embarrassed he

might be in front of the other fathers. What if his son were the only one to show up without a tie? How he looks is a reflection of how well I've lived up to my responsibility to teach him social skills. They'd think I'm a jerk. Doesn't he understand?

If father and son could talk it out more honestly, they still might not agree on *content.* The son would still think it ridiculous that it matters so much what a person wears. But in the *process* of discussing it he might be willing to make a compromise because it is so important to his dad.

The father won't change his mind about dressing properly for social occasions, but he might try to find a way to accommodate his son's feelings. Instead of insisting that his son wear a suit and tie, Dad might be satisfied if he at least wore slacks and a sport shirt. That way if some of the other guys were dressed casually, the son would still fit in.

The willingness to compromise can protect the integrity of the relationship. By respecting each other's feelings and needs, the father and son can create a win/win situation. Neither one of them needs to lose anything in the process.

When people can do that they create a safe, nurturing place where there is room for both of them and their different attitudes. Being able to reach that point would be the ideal resolution of your differences about bigotry.

Realistically, it may not happen. Depending on how bigoted your parents are, the issues you face will be more important than what to wear for dinner.

They might not let you bring your "other" friends home.

They might try to stop you from associating with them even away from home.

They might continue to try to influence you with their attitudes.

Depending on how often these issues arise and how many conflicts they cause, you may end up feeling responsible. For your own sake, you have to realize that your parents' bigotry is not your responsibility. It is their problem. You cannot change that, but you can make choices as to how you deal with it.

When a disagreement starts to turn into a full-scale battle, you can decide not to fight. You can pull back from the inclination to make one more point in your favor.

At first, that may seem a little strange. You may feel that you are giving up something, that somehow you are compromising your integrity.

That is a very common reaction. Most of us have been conditioned never to back down from anything. We have been told to stand up for ourselves, not to let anyone get the upper hand. But pulling away from a fight is not the same as backing down.

Fighting is a useful tool only when it solves the problem. If we know a solution is possible and we refuse to fight because we are scared, that is backing down. If we refuse to fight because there is no solution, it is a different matter entirely.

Continuing a hopeless confrontation only causes more frustration and stress. It is far healthier to let it go and move on to something more positive.

Jimmy Hudson used this technique successfully. Whenever possible, he avoided the subject of his wife's heritage and religion. He also didn't let his family bait him into an argument. The *process* he chose was the path of least resistance, and by doing that there was more harmony within the family.

You can do the same thing. You can choose not to react to your parents' bigoted comments. Don't let them provoke you into an argument.

*   *   *

Something else you may have to deal with is how your parents' bigotry affects your feelings toward them. As discussed in earlier chapters, respect is an important part of good family relationships. What happens to our respect when our parents act out their bigotry?

That situation is like any other that reminds us that our parents are only human. They make mistakes, and they can be wrong. Each time that happens, our respect is diminished a little more.

Does that mean that you are in a hopeless situation? Not necessarily. It is possible to have a good relationship despite the differences that remain. The key is being able to separate your feelings about the person from your feelings about what he does. You love your parents. You just don't like their bigotry.

To maintain love and respect, you have to focus on the positives. Like Jimmy, you have to look for the good things about your parents and ignore the bad. Ignoring does not mean condoning. It is the same as parents who still love a child who is on drugs: They separate the issue of drugs from their feelings about the child.

That is not easy. Issues can make us almost crazy with anger and frustration, especially issues that are clearly wrong and that we cannot change. But if we do not let the anger control us, we can achieve that balance most of the time.

To bolster the positive side of your relationship with your parents, look for specific things that you *can* respect them for:

- Are they understanding about most other things?
- Do they provide a clean, comfortable home for you?
- Do they encourage and support you in your interests?

- Do they accept their responsibilities in life well?
- Are they kind and considerate to others?

Often when we are angry at someone we forget everything except what made us mad. We forget that the person is someone we usually like. We flare up at a friend who let us down and forget all the times he was there for us.

But when we make a conscious decision to turn our attention to the positives, the negatives have a way of diminishing. They don't go away; they just don't seem so important. Being able to do that is a good coping mechanism for all kinds of situations. If you master it well for one problem, it will help you in countless others.

Another problem you may face in dealing with your parents' bigotry is maintaining your own values. A time may come when you have to take a stand in opposition to them. That can be pretty scary and takes a great deal of personal courage.

For instance, what if you discovered that one of your teachers was discriminating against a minority student in your class? Knowing your parents' attitudes, you are sure they would prefer for you to ignore the situation. Perhaps you even mention it to them, and they say it is none of your business, or it couldn't be true.

You know it is true, however. You have even heard other kids talking about it. So one day you decide to do something about it even though you know how your parents will react. You approach the student council president, and together you work up a plan of action.

The plan might include preparing written documentation of the specific incidents of discrimination with statements from witnesses. When that is complete, you send copies to the principal of your school and the district administration offices. Perhaps that leads to a special school board meeting for review.

To complicate your problem further, perhaps your father is a member of the school board. Because of his attitudes, he will probably argue that there is no case of discrimination. It may even come to an open debate between the two of you.

Depending on the outcome, it could create great problems for you. Your father could be extremely angry, seeing your actions as a personal attack against him. It could even create an antagonism that drives a wedge between you.

Considering those risks, do you still take this action that you feel is right?

Obviously, that is a question you will have to answer for yourself. No one can make the decision for you.

Taking an unpopular stand can be quite a challenge, especially when it is against your parents. It can make you feel like a traitor in a way: They have given you so much, and now you're going against them. You may even come to wonder if you are really right.

Perhaps it would help to know that you are not alone. Many other people have faced the same dilemma. Sometimes the outcome is of little social significance, affecting few more than the people directly involved. At other times it has considerable significance.

Martin Luther King, Jr. faced just such a dilemma in his struggle for civil rights. In direct opposition to his father's attitudes, King chose to see whites as potential friends instead of "the enemy." He even chose to trust some white politicians when that was an unpopular thing to do.

Every time the movement suffered a setback, King's father reminded him how wrong it was to believe in the whites.

King's unpopular stand also alienated him from many other blacks. Because he promoted peaceful, nonviolent protest, he was often ridiculed as too soft by some black leaders. Eventually that led to a split in the movement itself, when militant leaders formed activist groups promoting black power.

King's philosophy never again gained full support from the other black leaders, but his father eventually came around. Following a series of incidents in 1960, the elder King had to admit that some white politicians sincerely cared about equality and justice.

It began when King was arrested with student protesters in Atlanta. The mayor of Atlanta negotiated an agreement with the protesters: They were released and in return they agreed to stop the sit-ins while the mayor talked to local merchants about desegregating the lunch counters.

When the students were released, King was not. A local judge had discovered that King was on probation for a traffic violation—driving without a valid Georgia license. After a short trial on charges of probation violation, the judge sentenced King to four months at hard labor at the state penitentiary at Reidsville.

King was taken to Reidsville before he could even file an appeal. News of that unfair treatment spread quickly. Eventually it reached the office of then Presidential candidate John F. Kennedy. Kennedy's brother, Robert, called the judge and persuaded him to release King on bail until the case could be appealed.

King returned home, and his father became a supporter of Kennedy for President.

Oddly enough, the Kennedys' support of King was another example of courage. In the early '60s civil rights was still an unpopular cause. For the Kennedys to back King publicly could have been politically devastating.

*   *   *

Another example of someone's standing up for the right against incredible odds comes from fiction. *The Adventures of Huckleberry Finn* has long been criticized as a racist book filled with language highly offensive to blacks. But Clay Reynolds, associate professor and novelist in residence at the University of North Texas, in Denton, does not consider it a racist book. In a column written for the Dallas *Morning New*, he wrote, "It may be one of the most profoundly moving stories of communication and understanding between blacks and whites ever written in America."

In addressing the complaints against the book, Reynolds said that too often people fail to recognize the real message. All they see is a presentation of slavery and black-white relations in the worst possible light. They don't see the "tremendous power that rests in Huck's ultimate decision to forfeit his immortal soul rather than send Jim back to slavery and certain punishment."

"For Huck to damn his soul to save a slave in the 1840s was no idle act of heroism. It frightens him, and the decision forms the climax of the book, the point of the tale. It also underscores the depth of understanding Huck comes to during his river adventure in the company of a man he had teased and tortured and comes to love for not merely his personality but also for his humanity, for the depth and genuineness of his soul."

In the story, Huck risked a great deal more than the anger of his parents. Aiding a fugitive slave was a criminal offense, and it was a tremendous act of courage for Huck to make the decision he made. The fact that he could do that knowing the risks he faced is a fine example for the rest of us.

Something else significant about the book is that it deals

with real truth. It is an ugly truth. The way blacks were treated at that time was despicable, and white attitudes were nothing to be proud of. It is hard to look at that kind of truth. It would be easier to put it away and forget about it. But as Clay Reynolds says, "Through painful awareness of truth, power for change often can be obtained . . ."

It is that painful awareness that will dictate to each of us when to take a stand for something we believe in: when we know deep in our heart that the wrong cannot continue; when we know deep in our heart that we have to do something about it.

CHAPTER 14

Hope for the Future

"Until justice is blind to color, until education is unaware of race, until opportunity is unconcerned with the color of men's skins, emancipation will be a proclamation, not a fact. To the extent that the proclamation is not fulfilled in fact, to that extent we shall have fallen short of assuring freedom to the free."
                                        —Lyndon B. Johnson

On one hand, that statement seems to imply that we are hopelessly mired in problems of racism. But although it does have an undercurrent of pessimism, it is also a beacon of hope for the future. If we could achieve the objectives as former President Johnson stated them, we would be rid of the evil of bigotry.

To understand the pessimism, perhaps we should also put the quotation in its proper time period. Johnson spoke during a memorial service observing the centennial of the Battle of Gettysburg, in May 1963. At the time, Johnson was Vice-President, and the civil rights movement was just gaining strength. There was still an awful lot of ground to cover.

Comparing then to now, it is clear that a great deal of progress has been made. Segregation has all but disappeared. Educational and job opportunities for minorities have improved, and greater numbers of minorities are moving out of inner-city poverty and enjoying a better life-style.

Legislation and government programs were responsible for many of these advances. But Gordon Allport is of the opinion that the programs would not have worked if people in general had not supported them. He believes that racial prejudice has decreased in recent history because of several factors:

More interracial contact. The more we associate with other ethnic groups in school, at work, and in social settings, the more we can find the common ground that can pull us together. Getting to know each other destroys the stereotypes and discourages separateness.

But just throwing people together without a plan of action does not work. Coming together as groups can work only if we all make a personal commitment to the goal. If we want to achieve racial harmony, we have to be willing to accept people for themselves and to truly respect the things that make us different.

Decreased sense of class difference. Racial prejudice is strongly influenced by differences in social class. Conditions will improve as more minorities become socially equal and no longer feel oppressed. Here, too, the more we have in common with each other, the greater the possibility that we can accept each other.

Higher overall educational level. To quote a popular television slogan, "The more we know, the better off we are." That pretty well says it all. For too long bigotry was supported by simple ignorance of any other way. People accepted it. Now the general public has the advantage of educational backgrounds that help to question the status quo.

Many people, however, when asked their opinion about problems with bigotry and racism, still say, "What problems?" In their minds the problems have been solved. They point out the civil rights laws that have passed, the progress in overall assimilation, and they wonder what all the flap is about.

But as Gordon Allport explains, "Legal action has only an indirect bearing on the reduction of personal prejudice. Law is intended only to control the outward expression of intolerance."

Allport goes on to say that eventually the control of actions can have an effect on prejudicial feelings and attitudes. For that reason, he lists legislation as a major factor in the fight against bigotry. But it cannot win the battle alone.

Despite all our apparent progress, problems with racism still exist across the country, and it takes only one action to ignite the fire. One day everything is calm and peaceful; the next day a tense atmosphere of frustration and anger is created by a single incident.

It was just such an incident that fueled a near-crisis in Dallas in November, 1990. An off-duty police officer, Robert Bernal, had a major confrontation with County Commissioner John Wiley Price. The confrontation involved an ill-advised remark by Bernal, to which Price reacted by chasing the officer with a weapon.

Luckily, no one was hurt, at least not physically, and the matter was resolved as satisfactorily as it could have been, considering that no one was right. But the interesting thing about the incident is what caused it.

It was not just Bernal's remark, or even Price's reaction. It was an accumulation of frustration and anger on both sides.

According to Henry Tatum, associate editor of the Dallas *Morning News* editorial page, what happened between Bernal and Price was only a symptom, and the illness will not be cured by just treating the symptoms. "Part of the illness is caused by unemployment, poverty, deteriorating neighborhoods that too many people have been locked into, while too many other people don't seem to care."

Another part of the illness is the misconception that the problems are all caused by whites. It is almost as if people believe that all the problems will go away if the white folks just get it together. But Don Williamson, a columnist for the Seattle *Times*, does not agree. He believes that "working to understand another race is a two-way street."

Williamson makes the point that all the attention is on understanding minorities, with little emphasis on minorities understanding whites. Mutual lack of understanding is why we have so much insensitivity on both sides. Williamson says, "A lot of that insensitivity comes from so many of us spending so much time segregating ourselves that we never learned how to treat each other like human beings."

John Wiley Price is a good example of that. His actions and reactions clearly indicate that he sees whites as "the enemy." He is fairly militant in attitude and quick to label every incident as racist. His motives are good—he sincerely wants to improve conditions—but his means are suspect, even among other blacks.

It is interesting to note that considerable difference in

attitude exists between suburban blacks and inner-city blacks. Inner-city blacks, like Price, still cling to the litany of injustices since slavery. Suburban blacks seem to be able to get past that.

Barry believes that is probably true in general. He says that most of his black friends at a suburban school are pretty tolerant of whites. "No one seems to have an attitude problem," he says. "Sure, we're sensitive to racial remarks, but we don't assume that every white guy has something against us."

To find out more about the difference between black opinions, Jessica conducted her own informal experiment. Most of her association with blacks had been in suburbia, and as she explains, "We're all sort of sheltered here. We see only one part of what it means to be black."

In the past year Jessica has started going into the inner city to meet other blacks. She discovered that many of them did have an instant attitude against whites. They questioned why she was there and were reluctant to believe she was just interested.

She also learned two terms used to distinguish suburban and city blacks. *Weathermen* refers to blacks who have grown up with all the advantages of suburban life. As Jessica puts it, "They're like everyone else except they've got a little darker tan." *Downtown* refers to the inner-city blacks who are still struggling against barriers to growth. They are often more militant than others and sometimes have an attitude against the weathermen.

The blacks who harbor hostile attitudes against whites justify them the same way white supremacists justify their attitudes. Both are equally misguided and often unaware of how much they contribute to the problems.

These attitudes and how we react to them can stand in the way of improving race relations.

An experience that Danielle had is a good example. Until she went to first grade, she had not seen many black people. Her teacher was black, and Danielle was intrigued by the new experience. One day, out of curiosity, Danielle asked the teacher why she was called "black" when her skin was really brown. The teacher found the question offensive and insisted that Danielle apologize. She also didn't answer the question.

Since Danielle had meant nothing wrong, she didn't think she had to apologize. "I ended up getting a spanking over it," she says.

The incident illustrates how certain attitudes can cause behavior that is hard to understand, which then creates hard feelings. Often it is also behavior that is contrary to what the person is really like.

Danielle says that the teacher was very nice most of the time, and they had no problems. Now she understands that the teacher's response was pure reaction. It the teacher had stopped to think, she might have handled it differently.

A flip side to that situation is an incident related by Susan.

"My mother grew up in a little town in the South, and her family was quite comfortable financially. Mother was always dressed in pretty white dresses with her hair fixed real nice. She was also used to going places with her parents all the time.

"One day when she was about five, her father took her to the drugstore for a soda. Next to her at the counter was a black man. When his food was served, my mother asked him why he didn't wash his hands; they were dirty.

"First the man laughed. Then he said that he had washed his hands. He turned them palm up so she could see that the insides were clean and almost as white as hers.

Then he explained that the dark part was just the natural color of his skin and wouldn't wash off.

"That really made an impression on my mother. She grew up with a positive attitude because of that man's kind response. She then passed that attitude on to us."

We cannot ignore the fact that the negative attitudes of blacks are based on some truth. Whites have discriminated against them. However, it does not make them right and us wrong. Placing blame, pointing fingers, only increases the problems. As long as we continue to stand on opposites sides of an imaginary line that separates us, we will not progress much further than where we are.

Even though we have a long way to go, things have changed and people have changed. Sometimes the change seems painfully slow. Often it is overlooked in the attention given to steps taken backward, but evidence of change is all around us. And the greatest hope for the future rests with each person who is able to take his or her step forward.

How we choose to take our steps can greatly influence our effectiveness. Do we continue to draw battle lines and take sides against each other? Or do we try to find a better way?

During the turbulence of the 1950's and '60s when civil unrest swept the country, one voice of reason belonged to Martin Luther King, Jr. Offering his nonviolent philosophy of resistance to oppression, King captured the hearts of Americans of all colors. First he gave them a desire for change, and then the courage to effect that change.

King made people see that the civil rights movement was not just about homes and jobs and opportunities, but about *people*. He challenged the whites to look at the black man across the street and see a person, someone who shares their hopes, dreams, and concerns.

King also challenged the blacks to let go of their anger over past injustice. He did not tell them to forget it, or pretend it never happened. He simply encouraged them to look at the issues with reason and not to mistrust all white people.

Above all, King believed that good would win out, and he never deviated from that belief. Perhaps it would be fitting to close with his words:

"When evil men plot, good men must plan. When evil men burn and bomb, good men must build and bind. When evil men shout ugly words of hatred, good men must commit themselves to the glories of love. Where evil men would seek to perpetuate an unjust status quo, good men must seek to bring into being a real order of justice."

Appendices

APPENDIX A ORGANIZATIONS THAT OPPOSE BIGOTRY

A number of national and international organizations have long been working to eliminate prejudice and guarantee equality. The following are some of them:

The United States Civil Rights Commission was established in 1957 and reports to the President and Congress. It investigates civil rights complaints and collects and studies information on discrimination.

Many states, counties, and cities have special agencies to handle problems of discrimination in jobs, housing, and education. These agencies are usually called Human Relations Commission or Human Rights Commission. Listings for these organizations can be found in local telephone directories.

The Anti-Defamation League of B'nai B'rith, 823 United Nations Plaza, NY 10017, is a private organization whose main goal is to educate the public about cultural differences and promote positive human relations. Founded in 1913 during a time when anti-Semitism was blatant, the ADL was considered a watchdog for Jewish concerns. Its focus has broadened to include all kinds of bigotry.

Another group that has worked for individual rights for a long time is the American Civil Liberties Union (ACLU), 132 West 43rd Street, NY 10036. Members believe that abuses of government power and violations of a person's rights can destroy liberty for all people. Because of the belief, they are not affiliated with specific ethnic groups. They work to protect personal liberty for people of any race or culture.

The National Association for the Advancement of Colored People (NAACP), 4805 Mt. Hope Drive, Baltimore MD 21215, is perhaps the oldest civil rights organization. It has had a great impact on such issues as voting rights, job discrimination, and segregation.

An organization set up to protect the rights of another minority group is the American-Arab Anti-Discrimination Committee (ADC), 1731 Connecticut Ave. NW, Washington DC 20009. Through this organization Arab-Americans protest stereotypes and slurs in the media and elsewhere. The ADC also works to eliminate discrimination in jobs and education.

Amnesty International, 322 Eighth Ave., NY 10001, is a well-known international organization that works to protect human rights. Based in London, it has affiliate groups in 140 countries. It concentrates on "prisoners of conscience," people who have been jailed because of their beliefs.

Other organizations include:

Asian-American Legal Defense and Education Fund
99 Hudson Street
New York, NY 10013

Chinese for Affirmative Action
17 Walter U. Lum Place
San Francisco, CA 94108

Congress of Racial Equality (CORE)
236 West 116th Street
New York, NY 10026

Indian Rights Association
1505 Race Street
Philadelphia, PA 19102

Klanwatch Project of the Southern Poverty Law Center
400 Washington Street
Montgomery, AL 36101

NAACP Legal Defense and Education Fund, Inc.
99 Hudson Street
New York, NY 10013

National Gray Panthers
311 South Juniper Street
Philadelphia, PA 19107

National Institute against Prejudice and Violence
525 West Redwood Street
Baltimore, MD 21201

National Jewish Community Relations Advisory Council
443 Park Avenue
New York, NY 10016

National Legal Aid and Defender Association
1625 K Street NW
Washington, DC 20006

National Organization for Women (NOW)
1401 New York Avenue NW
Washington, DC 20005-2102

National Urban League, Inc.
500 East 62nd Street
New York, NY 10021

People for the American Way
1424 16th Street NW
Washington, DC 20036

Puerto Rican Legal Defense and Educational Fund
99 Hudson Street
New York, NY 10013

Most of these organizations have chapters nationwide and can be located through the local telephone directory.

APPENDIX B   TYPES OF DISCRIMINATION

Discrimination is not limited to the United States. It happens around the world, and it is not always just a private, individual choice. The United Nations classes discrimination in two categories, private and public.

Private discrimination is when one person decides not to sell his house to another person because of prejudicial attitudes. Public discrimination is when the decision is based on *official* rulings or is government-sanctioned.

Among the forms of discrimination *officially* practiced in various parts of the world, the United Nations lists the following:

1. Unequal recognition before the law (general denial of rights to particular groups).
2. Inequality of personal security (interference, arrest, disparagement because of group membership).
3. Inequality in freedom of movement and residence (ghettos, forbidden travel, prohibited areas, curfew restrictions).
4. Inequality in protection of freedom of thought, conscience, or religion.
5. Inequality in the enjoyment of free communication.
6. Inequality in the right of peaceful association.
7. Inequality in the treatment of those born out of wedlock.
8. Inequality in the enjoyment of the right to marry and found a family.
9. Inequality in the enjoyment of a free choice of employment.
10. Inequality in the regulation and treatment of ownership.

11. Inequality in the protection of authorship.
12. Inequality of opportunity for education or the development of ability or talent.
13. Inequality of opportunity for sharing the benefits of culture.
14. Inequality in services rendered (health protection, recreational facilities, housing).
15. Inequality in the enjoyment of the right to nationality.
16. Inequality in the right to participate in government.
17. Inequality in access to public office.
18. Forced labor, slavery, special taxes, the forced wearing of distinguishing marks, sumptuary laws, and public libel of groups.

Bibliography

Allport, Gordon. *The Nature of Prejudice*. New York: Addison-Wesley, 1986.

Aronson, Elliot. *The Social Animal*. New York: W.H. Freeman & Co., 1988.

Bloomfield, Harold, MD, with Leonard Felder, PhD. *Making Peace with Your Parents*. New York: Random House, 1983.

Campbell, Angus. *White Attitudes toward Black People*. Ann Arbor: Institute for Social Research, University of Michigan, 1971.

Clark, Kenneth B. *Prejudice and Your Child*. Boston: Beacon Press, 1963.

Cook, Fred J. *The Ku Klux Klan: America's Recurring Nightmare*. New York: Julian Messner, 1980.

Darby, Jean. *Martin Luther King Jr*. Minneapolis: Lerner Publications Co., 1990.

Ehrlich, Paul R., and Feldman, S. Shirley. *The Race Bomb*. New York: New York Times Book Co., 1977.

Gay, Kathlyn. *Bigotry*. New Jersey: Enslow Publishers, Inc., 1989.

Helmreich, William B. *The Things They Say behind Your Back: Stereotypes and the Myths behind Them*. New York: Doubleday, 1982.

Jakoubek, Robert. *Martin Luther King, Jr*. New York: Chelsea House Publishers, 1989.

Jordan, Winthrop D. *The White Man's Burden*. New York: Oxford University Press, 1974.

King, Martin Luther, Jr. *The Words of Martin Luther King, Jr.*, selected by Coretta Scott King. New York: Newmarket Press, 1983.

Levine, Robert S., and Campbell, Donald T. *Ethnocentrism— Theories of Conflict, Ethnic Attitude & Group Behavior.* New York: John Wiley & Sons, 1972.

Lieberman, Mendel, and Hardie, Marion. *Resolving Family and Other Conflicts: Everybody Wins.* Unity Press.

Miller, Arthur G. *In the Eye of the Beholder: Contemporary Issues in Stereotyping.* New York: Praeger Publishers, 1982.

Rowland, Della. *Martin Luther King Jr., The Dream of Peaceful Revolution.* New Jersey: Silver Burdett Press, 1990.

Index